A SEMINAR GAME TO ANALYZE REGIONAL GOVERNANCE OPTIONS FOR PORTUGAL

T0159715

James P. Kahan

Mirjam van het Loo

Manuela Franco

João Gomes Cravinho

Vasco Rato

João Tiago Silveira

Fátima Fonseca

Supported by
RAND Europe and
The Luso-American Foundation for Development

RAND EUROPE

PREFACE

The Luso-American Foundation for Development (FLAD, for its Portuguese name), true to its vocation as a promoter of scientific knowledge and socio-economic progress in Portugal, decided to conduct a prospective study of regionalization in Portugal, simulating scenarios of life in 2010 according to some of the likely possible options. FLAD carried out the study in cooperation with, and with the support of RAND. The aim was not only to help clarify some of the aspects and implications of an important, but complex, problem, but also to introduce to Portugal an innovative methodology which has shown highly promising results in other areas.

The aim of the study is much more than mere research into an individual case. The idea is, by examining a concrete situation, to illustrate the advantage of being able to evaluate public policies as objectively as possible. It also demonstrates the absence of private organizations in Portugal—although there are no public ones either—capable of conducting this kind of research in a scientific manner.

Anyone who is familiar with the methods of evaluating public policies used since the end of World War II, first in the United States and Canada and later in some European countries (Norway, the Netherlands and Denmark and now in France, Great Britain and Switzerland), will recognize that is has been mainly in public institutions—budget control departments and audit offices—that these methodologies have been applied. We are also aware that, without private, independent bodies capable of applying and developing evaluation techniques, scientific progress would not have been possible. Neither would it have been possible to guarantee results that were credible and free from any political manipulation.

Portugal has to keep up with this great movement towards rationalization and objectivity in evaluating public policies and to draw people's attention to the vacuum that exists at present. A highly constructive step would be to give a concrete example of the use and value of these methods of evaluation.

Having done the study, one has to recognise that it was a worthwhile experience. True, no clear and definitive answers about the best concrete solution for Portugal were presented—but that is neither the objective nor the main purpose of this methodology. The simulation allowed those who participated at the seminar games, as it will now allow those who will read this report, to get a deeper insight into the question "Should administrative regions be created in Portugal?" shedding new light on the subject. Common sense pointed to the existence of some consensus on a number of issues: the absolute need for decentralisation, bringing government closer to the people; the refusal to increase bureaucracy, the number of civil servants and politicians and the explicit refusal to raise new taxes; the need to preserve the values of existing local government; and a reluctance to discuss the regional issue in a vague or ideological fashion, without considering the actual responsibilities or the costs involved. That consensus has been further strengthened.

The reader should now be able to judge these issues for himself on the merits of this work.

> Rui Chancerelle de Machete
> President of the Executive Council, FLAD
> Lisboa, Portugal

****

This report, prepared for FLAD, describes the background, methods, results and conclusions from a series of four seminar games conducted by RAND Europe in June 1998 to examine alternative strategies of decentralization of the Portuguese government. The primary purpose of the report was to inform the debate surrounding the referendum of 8 November 1998 on whether to install a regional administrative layer of government in the country. The report should be of interest to persons concerned with Portugal, with regionalization of government competencies and with gaming as a policy analytic tool.

A companion volume, *Documentation of a Seminar Game to Analyze Regional Governance Options for Portugal* (RAND Europe Report RE 98.017.2) contains all of the materials presented to the participants and the summary notes of the team working sessions and the wrapup session. All of these materials are in the Portuguese language. This volume is available from RAND Europe or FLAD upon request.

A Seminar Game to Analyze Regional Governance Options for Portugal was prepared by RAND Europe, the European subsidiary of RAND. The director of RAND Europe is Richard Fallon. Communications regarding this report may be addressed to him:

Richard Fallon, Ph.D.
RAND Europe
Newtonweg 1
2333 CP Leiden
The Netherlands
Telephone: +31-71-524.51.51
Fax: +31-71-524.51.91

TABLE OF CONTENTS

SUMMARY

REGIONALIZATION IN PORTUGAL

On 8 November 1998, the Portuguese people will be asked to vote on a referendum concerning the introduction of a regional administrative layer of government, between the national and municipal levels. The referendum will pose two questions:

1. Do you agree with the concrete plan to institute administrative regions?
2. Do you agree with the concrete plan to institute an administrative region in the area where you vote?

The first question refers indirectly to Law 56/91, which called for the establishment of regional assemblies, partially elected by direct vote and partially appointed by the municipal governments in the region. The regional assemblies would have no legislative powers, but would appoint and ratify the decisions of a regional administration. Law 56/91 transfers from the national administration to these to-be-created regional administrations competencies in 12 areas, namely:
- Economic and social development;
- Spatial planning;
- Environment, nature preservation and water management;
- Transport and communication infrastructure;
- Housing;
- Education and vocational training;
- Culture and national heritage;
- Youth, sports and leisure;
- Tourism;
- Public utilities;
- Agricultural support; and
- Municipal support.

The second question refers directly to Law 19/98, which divides mainland Portugal into eight regions within which Law 56/91 will be implemented. This question asks the voters in each proposed region whether they approve of that area actually being established as an administrative region. These eight regions are:
- *Região de Entre Douro e Minho*
- *Região de Trás-os-Montes e Alto Douro*
- *Região da Beira Litoral*
- *Região da Beira Interior*
- *Região da Estremadura e Ribatejo*
- *Região de Lisboa e Setúbal*
- *Região do Alentejo*
- *Região do Algarve*

This referendum is the culmination of many years of discussion and debate within Portugal on the subject of regional government. Although Portugal has been highly centralized throughout the twentieth century (as well as before), regions have been contemplated throughout this time, and actual regional planning goes back to the 1950s. Following the sweeping democratic reforms begun in the 1970s and the entry of Portugal into the European Union in the 1980s, the impetus for some form of decentralization mounted steadily. There is general acknowledgment of the need for a more active role for citizenship and for the values and practices associated with it, in keeping with public opinion, which is increasingly vocal in its demands. Thus, the debate is not about decentralization—which almost everybody believes necessary—but about the best way to achieve decentralization. A major watershed in the debate about the best way to achieve decentralization occurred in August 1991, when the National Assembly passed Law 56/91. This law placed a concrete form of regionalization on the table, which became the focus of the decentralization debate. After years of consideration, the proposal of Law 56/91 is finally facing a decisive moment in the referendum.

The concrete proposals of Laws 56/91 and 19/98 by no means provide a fully described implementation plan for regionalization. There is a significant question in the minds of many Portuguese voters of what this change in governance would mean. The arguments invoked in favor of or against regionalization often sound the same. Although the referendum debate is beginning to follow party lines, with the PS (Socialist Party) sponsoring advertisements for a "yes" vote and the PSD (Social Democratic Party) sponsoring advertisements for voting "no," prominent people across the political spectrum can be found in both camps. A third camp, also containing many supporters, argues that the referendum itself is flawed because the questions posed are poorly formulated.

A SEMINAR GAME TO INFORM THE DEBATE

In this political environment—where there is diversity of opinion but little consensus on the outcomes of the policy choice—the use of seminar gaming to explore the possibilities of different regionalization alternatives is attractive. A comparison of informed opinions of how Portugal might function under several proposed decentralization schemes might inform the regionalization debate by providing a more concrete picture of the likely results of adopting the proposal of Laws 56/91 and 19/98 or alternative means of decentralization. At the request of the Luso-American Foundation for Development (FLAD, for its Portuguese name), RAND Europe designed and conducted a series of such seminar games, which took place in four Portuguese cities (Lisboa, Évora, Viseu, and Porto) in June 1998.

Seminar gaming was chosen as the method of approach because it provides a means of marshalling the inherent expertise of groups of participants to understand complex societal problems. The groups are placed in a "scenario"—or depiction of a possible future—and asked critical questions which permit an exploration of policies proposed to solve the problems. There are thus three central attributes to a seminar game: (1) the participants and how they are grouped into "teams," (2) the scenario that is presented, and (3) the activities the participants engage in.

Participants

Participants for the seminar game were recruited from the four target cities by contacting key private individuals and local officials. A broad spectrum of mid-level people were sought, to represent local government, local representatives of the central government, service providers, entrepreneurs, labor unions, academics, and professionals. An effort was made to recruit women, young people, and older people, as well as people who might be expected to have differing positions in the debate on how best to decentralize. In all 21 people from each of the four cities agreed to participate, and 83 people in all actually participated in the seminar games. Among these participants, all the desired representation was obtained with the exception that fewer women and older people than planned could be recruited.

The design, conduct and analysis of the seminar games was done by a "control team" of two RAND Europe researchers and five Portuguese counterparts; these latter people occupied the formal roles during the game sessions. The game director and assistant have expertise and experience in Portuguese government and law. They were supplemented by three game rapporteurs who are junior university professors in law, international relations and economics and themselves have experience in government. The control team benefited from consultations before and after the games with FLAD officials and an Advisory Board consisting of senior people from the academic and political worlds.

Scenarios

The scenario materials we designed can be divided into two groups, which we have termed the "external" scenario and the "decentralization" scenario. Two different forms of the external scenario were constructed, to represent a future world of Portuguese and European prosperity and economic downturn, respectively. The seminar game sessions in Lisboa and Viseu employed the prosperous scenario while the seminar game sessions in Évora and Porto employed the depressed one.

Three different forms of the decentralization scenario were constructed, representing respectively (1) a "yes" vote on the referendum, leading to the implementation of Laws 56/91 and 19/98, (2) a "no" vote on the referendum, leading to devolution of central competencies to municipalities, and (3) a cancellation of the referendum and establishment of regional centers for coordinated decisionmaking, whose membership was appointed by the municipalities.

External scenarios. The two external scenarios presented pictures of Portugal and Europe in 2010 enjoying a prolonged period of economic prosperity or suffering the "Euro-depression of 2007," respectively. This was accomplished by providing information on the following subjects:

- General information on the functioning of the European Union and the Economic and Monetary Union and on the relationship between Portugal and the European Union.
- The economic situation in Portugal.
- The demographic situation in Portugal.
- Developments in major policy areas. Information was provided on health care, social security, education, environment, infrastructure, telecommunications and housing.

Decentralization scenarios. There were three decentralization scenarios, representing three different ways of dealing with the perceived need to reduce the degree of centralization of Portuguese governance. Participants at each seminar game session were divided into three teams, and each team was given a different decentralization scenario. The teams were drawn up to be as similar to each other as possible, each having members from the different categories used for recruiting. Each scenario began with a reference to the planned regionalization referendum, went on to describe in general terms the subsequent consequences, and then described how the twelve competency areas for regions specified in Law 56/91 plus the thirteenth area of health were managed. In each of the decentralization scenarios, it was stated that the implementation was done in good faith, in order to provide as efficient and effective a government responsive to the public as possible.

- **Scenario A: "Yes" on the referendum.** This scenario followed the language of Law 56/91 very closely. The specification of competencies was drawn from descriptions published in Portuguese newspapers by advocates of regionalization.

- **Scenario B: "No" on the referendum.** This scenario took as its premise that the defeat of the referendum discredited regional governance. Instead, many of the competencies of the central government devolved to the municipalities. Although there were no formal regional organs of government, the municipalities self-organized on an issue-by-issue basis to better coordinate their efforts.

- **Scenario C: Regional decision centers.** This scenario attempted to provide an alternative that provided for some regional autonomy, but did not have the specific structure of Law 56/91 or the eight regions of Law 19/98. In this scenario, seven regional decision centers were created, representing the two metropolitan areas of Lisboa and Porto plus the five central coordinating regions (CCRs) currently in place for Portugal's economic and social regional development programs with the European Union. Instead of the regional assembly mechanism, the members of the decision centers were appointed by municipalities proportionally to their population. Competencies in most of the 12 areas specified by Law 56/91 plus health were transferred from the central government to these bodies, but to a slightly lesser extent than in Scenario A. Ministerial administrative offices outside of the capital were replaced by regional offices in the seven regional chief cities.

Activities

A day at a seminar game. Each game lasted an entire day, beginning at about 9:00 and lasting until after 18:00. The external scenario, representing Portugal on 30 April 2010, was presented to the entire group, after which the participants were divided into three teams, each of which was given a different decentralization scenario. Participants discussed the scenario for five hours (with a long break for lunch), following a format of structured questions. To conclude the day, the participants were brought back together into a single group to compare their experiences under the different decentralization scenarios and to discuss some more general issues.

Team tasks. The major work of the teams was to discuss their scenarios in order to answer specific questions posed to them. A common set of questions was used for all three teams, broken into four question sets.

- **Set 1:** The nature and allocation of government financing for different levels of government.
- **Set 2:** Key characteristics of the functioning of the Portuguese government, including the degree of bureaucratization and regulation, the responsiveness of the government to the citizens' needs, access of citizens to the needed services, the need for coordination within the Portuguese government and the complexity of policy formulation and implementation.
- **Set 3:** The way in which the government will deal with specific competencies; specific areas queried included education, environment, health care and disaster management.
- **Set 4:** The strengths and weaknesses of the scenario from the viewpoint of different interest groups, including small and medium enterprises, large industrial firms, unskilled and semi-skilled laborers, retirees and people desiring to preserve the Portuguese culture and national heritage.

Closing session. In the final closing session, the rapporteurs informed all the participants about the nature of all three decentralization scenarios and a discussion was held to compare the experience of the three teams on:

- The functioning of the Portuguese government (largely following question set 2, above).
- The qualifications government personnel needed for effective decentralization.
- Issues regarding coordination with the European Union.
- Areas in which competencies should be centralized and areas in which competencies should be decentralized.

RESULTS

From the record of activities of the four seminar game sessions, nine major themes were identified. Some of the themes represent issues which were brought out in most (if not all) team discussions; others differed in relevance or nature for different scenarios or in different game locales.

- A: Effect of the external scenarios;
- B: Acceptance of the decentralization scenarios;
- C: The importance of decentralization;
- D: The best way to decentralize;
- E: Distribution and coordination of responsibilities;
- F: National government as the center of gravity in collection and distribution of financial resources;
- G: What is the appropriate way to distribute financial resources over different layers of government?
- H: Distribution of human resources over different layers of government;
- I: National solidarity.

A. Effect of the external scenarios

The external scenarios were presented to the players as plausible pictures of Portugal in 2010 and there was a general acceptance of them. There was not too great of a difference in the results of the seminar games using the prosperous scenario from those presented the Euro-depression. Teams confronted with a depressed economy had a slightly more strained atmosphere during their deliberations; resources were not readily available to resolve problems or find compromises among different participant positions. Teams confronted with prosperity, on the other hand, were more relaxed and showed less concern about policy issues. Difficulties were solved whenever possible by spending money.

B. Acceptance of the decentralization scenarios

In contrast to the external scenarios, there were some objections to the decentralization scenarios. Generally, people were willing to accept Scenario A. Although the general concept of Scenario B was acceptable, there was sometimes difficulty accepting competencies devolving to municipalities. While the cancellation of the referendum and the concept of the regional decision centers of Scenario C met with no objection, some participants found that the scenario was not well-enough specified to assess and did not understand how it was intended to work. Although specific elements of each scenario (for example, specifics regarding competencies) encountered resistance from time to time, these elements varied from game session to game session. Overall, it is legitimate to conclude that the decentralization scenarios were accepted.

C. The importance of decentralization

Participants were explicit and virtually unanimous in their declaration that some decentralization of competencies is very important and necessary. The present Portuguese government was viewed as too centralist and no longer (if it ever was) the appropriate way to deal with problems in society. These emerged in all four game sessions and in all decentralization scenarios. No matter what form of decentralization a participant might have believed is best, the actual form used in his or her decentralization scenario was preferred to no decentralization at all.

This said, the participants also pointed out that decentralization had potential negative side-effects to be guarded against. Decentralization might make it more difficult to accomplish structural changes and to formulate national policies. Some policies with national implications (for example, foreign relations, air quality) or areas having conflicts of interest within Portugal might best remain centralized.

D. The best way to decentralize

Although there was clear agreement on the question whether decentralization should take place, there was no agreement among the participants on what the best form of decentralization might be. There did not emerge, either during the team sessions or in the final general session, any consensus as to whether Scenario A (a "yes" vote) or Scenario B (a "no" vote) was the better choice. Scenario C (regional decision centers) was not as well-regarded as the other because participants saw no clear structure in that scenario and consequently could not easily envision its benefits.

When participants expressed a preference for regional administration (Scenario A), the most-often cited reason was efficient decentralization of national competencies. When participants expressed a preference for devolution (Scenario B), the most-often cited reason was because municipalities and parishes know better what the people want. But more important than either of these positions was the consensus that there was a need for clarity in the way in which any particular form of decentralization would be implemented, and that this clarity was lacking from the debate on the referendum.

E. Distribution and coordination of responsibilities

The participants saw a need for coordination of government policies and there was a consensus expressed that a clear definition of responsibilities is an important condition for efficient and effective coordination. The participants also saw that this clear definition was missing, both within the confines of the seminar game and in the larger public discussion from which the seminar game derived.

Although most of the public discussion on governmental coordination with respect to decentralization has concentrated on vertical coordination (from central to local, possibly with regions), the participants also brought out the need for horizontal coordination—among regions or among municipalities. In the referendum debate, neither side attends adequately to horizontal coordination and in seminar game Scenario C, whose primary feature was such coordination, the information provided was not seen as specific enough. The participants believe that what is needed is a careful consideration of horizontal coordination for each governmental competency considered for decentralization; different competencies will require different degrees of horizontal coordination.

Participants also expressed the belief that the central government could gain in efficiency, effectiveness and quality if various services would be privatized (regardless of regionalization). It was viewed as important to determine which government tasks could be better done by organizations outside the government.

F. National government as the center of gravity in collection and distribution of financial resources

An obvious but important point brought out by the participants is that a precondition for effective decentralization is a substantial shift in public monies to local levels of government (meaning regions if they exist, municipalities, and parishes) is needed. There is a consensus over all three scenarios that there needs to be a formula determined at the national level to determine how much money each local unit will receive. This shift should occur by transferring more money from the national to sub-national levels of government rather than by permitting the sub-national levels of government to raise their own funds.

G. What is the appropriate way to distribute financial resources over different layers of government?

Although participants did not specify a national formula for distributing financial resources, they agreed that one should exist and that it should contain some kind of mechanism to correct for regional imbalances.

Whether a particular form of decentralization is good or not depends to a substantial extent on the way the local government will be financed. This means that a decentralization proposal offered to the country needs to contain some idea about how the national formula is determined, and what the guidelines for autonomy might be.

H. Distribution of human resources over different layers of government

Participants expressed the opinion that the quality of the government policy mainly depends on the quality of the people. When thinking about decentralization, it is important to consider what kind of personnel is needed on all levels of government and whether this personnel is available. Thus far, this topic has not received much public attention.

I. National solidarity

The participants agreed that regionalization should not lead to increasing differences among or within regions. They expressed some fear that differences among regions might increase in some areas such as the socio-economic status and the access to health care. Therefore, mechanisms should be put in place to ensure national solidarity and cohesion. If regionalization is to take place, then the central government has an important role in monitoring its effect and should act to mitigate inequities that might arise.

IMPLICATIONS FOR THE REGIONALIZATION DEBATE

The major objective of the seminar gaming exercise reported here is to inform the debate surrounding the forthcoming referendum on regionalization. Perhaps the most important finding in this regard is the often-stated remark by participants that improvements in the information supply with respect to the referendum are necessary. A number of participants criticized the government and the largest opposition party alike for poorly managing the referendum process. These critics stated that there has not yet been a serious debate on regionalization in Portugal, and the public has not yet been given sufficient information to make an informed choice.

These and other participants indicated that—in spite of the wording of the referendum and the interpretation of that wording stated by the Constitutional Court of Portugal—it is not clear to them what the actual proposal is. If these motivated and informed citizens hold such a belief, then the average voter, even trying to be informed, is not likely to know what he or she is voting for. A possible consequence is a high abstention rate, leading to an inconclusive result from the referendum.

Regionalization—yes or no?

A major finding of our study is that everybody seems to be in favor of decentralization. However, there is no consensus about whether decentralization should be accomplished by the implementation of the referendum proposal (Scenario A), direct devolution to municipalities (Scenario B) or horizontally coordinated regional decision centers (Scenario C). Before taking decisions on the best way to decentralize, it has to be clear which objectives are to be reached by the decentralization process. Subsequently, the type of decentralization that will most likely contribute to reaching those objectives may be chosen.

One issue to consider in this regard is the level of decentralization. Most governments have different organizational layers to which responsibilities can be transferred, meaning that government responsibilities can be decentralized in a variety of ways. In Portugal, a first option is to transfer powers from a national to a currently-existing local level (as in Scenario B). A second option is to transfer powers from the national government to one of the existing intermediate levels of government, i.e. to strengthen a currently-existing governmental entity between the national and current local levels. These could be an empowerment of the present 18 administrative districts or the present five CCRs (or their modification as in Scenario C). A third option is to establish a new layer of government to which responsibilities can be transferred (as in Scenario A). This question has been the central one in the regionalization debate in Portugal to date.

The seminar games indicated that the question may not be as critical as some people believe, in the sense that feasible ways to implement many different forms of decentralization are possible. The referendum is focused on only one particular form of decentralization—as embodied in Laws 56/91 and 19/88—and this is perhaps unfortunate. The details of that particular form, which include the number and location of the regions and the establishment of the directly elected regional assembly, mask the essential question of the functioning of any regional administrative body and how such a body would exercise its competencies and interact with both the central government and its constituent municipalities.

Knowledge to inform an electorate

Our answer to the question about regionalization in the subsection above is "it depends." Here, we indicate what it depends upon.

The devil is in the details. The seminar game made clear that the <u>implementation</u> of any decentralization scheme is at least as important as the actual characteristics of the scheme itself. Regionalization as a plan will succeed or fail depending on how it is implemented. Because the public is to be asked to give its opinion on the specific scheme of Laws 56/91 and 19/98 rather than on the abstract question of some form of regional administration, the implementation details must be provided to inform that vote. Proponents of the referendum should make clear which steps are to be taken and in what time frame. The schedule for devolving competencies and the horizontal and vertical coordination plans must be made explicit. And the financial structure to support all of this must be presented in detail.

Money does matter. One of the details not discussed in the present regionalization debate is how the new form of government will be financed. Our participants agreed that the financial structure of Portuguese taxation should not change, and that there should be a national formula to determine the share of each identified local unit. Moreover, they agreed that more money must be made available to local government to spend. While the details of the national formula (distribution plan) need not be part of the referendum debate, attention should be paid to the amount of money to be available to regional administration (and in turn to municipalities and parishes) and the autonomy in spending that money that the regional administrations would have. We also believe that the debate would benefit by the provision of a general philosophy to be used in drawing up the national formula for distribution. This philosophy should be explicit about the meaning of equity, the expectations placed upon richer and poorer regions, how special needs would be considered, and how adjustments might be made for economically good or bad times.

Competencies do matter. Ambiguities exist in the regionalization plan proposed in the referendum not only with respect to the allocation of financial resources, but also regarding how competencies would devolve. An important consideration here is the form of devolution. Decentralization of a specific responsibility to a specific layer of government can take different forms. The most important distinction is whether responsibilities are fully decentralized (autonomy) or are shared between different levels of government (shared responsibilities). This distinction needs to be explicit in the consideration of the role of a regional administration. The electorate would be well-served by more information regarding how competencies would be transferred to regions, including an overview of the coordination mechanisms for the different competencies, a plan for the distribution of financial and human resources and a consideration of mechanisms to fight the asymmetries that might result from regionalization.

Beyond the referendum

Even though there is a strong consensus for decentralization, we must caution that decentralization—via regionalization or other means—will not automatically have positive effects. Certain conditions need to be met to make decentralization succeed. These conditions (such as a clear division of responsibilities, a clear distribution of financial and human resources and national cohesion) were discussed above.

Whatever the outcome of the referendum, and whatever decentralization scheme is adopted by Portugal, a system needs to be put in place to evaluate the effects of decentralization. It is virtually certain that implementation will not be perfect—that some things will work well and others not so well. It could happen that decentralization has the desired consequences, but, in addition, has some foreseen or unforeseen negative side-effects. Mechanisms should be put in place to avoid or mitigate any negative direct effects or side-effects. An evaluation system, keyed to explicit objectives, will permit the monitoring of changes, and will permit Portugal to adaptively adjust its plan. If it turns out that regionalization indeed results in reaching the defined objectives, further steps to regionalize will be taken. If some (or all) objectives are not reached, perhaps alternative forms of decentralization for some competencies may need to be considered. By taking such an attentive, adaptive approach, Portugal can best ensure that decentralization is accomplished in an efficient, orderly manner.

RESUMO

A 8 de Novembro de 1998, os Portugueses vão ser chamados a referendar a instituição de regiões administrativas, que se apresentam como uma estrutura intermediária de poder, entre o governo central e os municípios. O referendo confrontará o eleitor com duas perguntas :

1. Concorda com a instituição em concreto das regiões administrativas?

2. Concorda com a instituição em concreto da região administrativa da sua área de recenseamento eleitoral?

A primeira pergunta refere-se indirectamente à lei 56/91, que prevê a instituição de Assembleias Regionais, eleitas em parte por sufrágio directo e em parte por representantes designados pelas Assembleias Municipais abrangidas pela região proposta. As Assembleias Regionais não dispõem de poder legislativo, mas têm a capacidade de eleger a Junta Regional e de se pronunciar sobre as respectivas decisões. Pela Lei 56/91 as eventuais regiões administrativas passarão a deter atribuições nas seguintes 12 áreas :
1. Desenvolvimento económico e social;
2. Ordenamento do território;
3. Ambiente, conservação da natureza e recursos hídricos;
4. Equipamento social e vias de comunicação;
5. Habitação;
6. Educação e formação profissional;
7. Cultura e património histórico;
8. Juventude, desporto e tempos livres;
9. Turismo;
10. Abastecimento público;
11. Apoio às actividades produtivas;

12. Apoio à acção dos municípios.

A segunda pergunta decorre directamente da Lei 19/98, que divide Portugal Continental em 8 Regiões, a instituir nos termos da Lei 56/91. Esta segunda pergunta pede aos eleitores que dêem o seu acordo à Região Administrativa proposta para a respectiva área de recenseamento. As Regiões previstas são as seguintes:
Região de Entre Douro e Minho;
Região de Trás-os-Montes e Alto Douro;
Região da Beira Litoral;
Região da Beira Interior;
Região da Estremadura e Ribatejo;
Região de Lisboa e Setúbal;
Região do Alentejo;
Região do Algarve.

Este referendo culmina um processo de muitos anos de discussão e debate sobre o tema da regionalização em Portugal. Sendo Portugal um Estado tradicionalmente centralizado, desde há muito que se contemplam hipóteses de criação de regiões e, na verdade, o planeamento regional data dos anos 50. Na sequência das reformas democráticas dos anos 70, e da entrada de Portugal na União Europeia, nos anos 80, a vontade de avançar com alguma forma de regionalização tem sido regularmente manifestada. Acresce que, em sintonia com uma opinião pública cada vez mais articuladas nas suas exigências, se verifica um reconhecimento crescente da importância de uma prática mais activa da cidadania e dos valores e comportamentos que lhe estão associados. Na verdade, pode dizer-se que o debate da regionalização não é tanto acerca da ideia de descentralizar - que quase todos julgam necessário - mas sobre a melhor maneira de o fazer.

A Lei 56/91, aprovada pela Assembleia da República em 1991, constituiu um passo importante neste debate: ao colocar na mesa uma proposta concreta de lei quadro das regiões administrativas, esta lei acabou por se tornar documento de referência no debate da regionalização. Ao serem submetidas a referendo, as propostas da lei 56/91 vão ser objecto de um teste decisivo, anos após a sua aprovação.

As propostas concretas das Leis 56/91 e 19/98 não fornecem nenhum plano pormenorizado para a concretização da regionalização. Na mente dos portugueses subsiste a interrogação sobre qual poderá ser o significado desta mudança do esquema de administração do poder. Frequentemente, os argumentos invocados a favor ou contra a regionalização assemelham-se. Apesar do debate do referendo estar marcado pelas linhas partidárias, são muitos os membros proeminentes da classe política que se dividem pelo sim e pelo não, à margem da posição defendida pelo partido político a que pertencem. Um terceiro campo, que também recolhe muitos apoios, argumenta que o próprio referendo é discutível por as perguntas não estarem capazmente formuladas.

UM SEMINÁRIO DE PROSPECTIVA PARA INFORMAR O DEBATE

Neste ambiente político - onde há diversidade de opinião mas fraco consenso sobre os resultados da escolha - pareceu interessante a hipótese de explorar as possibilidades das diferentes alternativas de regionalização através da realização de um Seminário de prospectiva. Uma comparação de opiniões informadas sobre o modo como Portugal funcionaria no quadro de diferentes modelos de descentralização poderia contribuir para informar o debate público, sobretudo se desse uma imagem mais concreta de possíveis resultados da adopção das propostas contidas nas Leis 56/91 e 19/98 ou de outras alternativas de descentralização. A pedido da Fundação Luso-Americana para o

Desenvolvimento, a RAND Europe desenhou uma série desses Seminários de prospectiva, que se realizaram em Lisboa, Évora, Viseu e Porto, em Junho 1998.

Os Seminários de prospectiva foram escolhidos como método de abordagem porque permitem congregar a experiência inerente a um dado grupo de participantes e usá-la para compreender problemas complexos da sociedade em que se inserem. Os grupos são colocados num "cenário" - ou descrição de um futuro possível - e confrontados com questões relevantes que permitem explorar as políticas propostas para resolver os problemas. Assim, num Seminário de prospectiva há três aspectos principais : 1) os participantes, e como são agrupados em equipas; 2) o cenário apresentado; e 3) as tarefas em que se envolvem os participantes.

Participantes

Os participantes nos Seminários foram recrutados nas quatro cidades designadas através de contactos estabelecidos com responsáveis locais e com pessoas envolvidas na vida da cidade ou nas áreas pré-definidas de recrutamento. Procurou-se um largo espectro de pessoas, de modo a recolher pontos de vista do poder local, de funcionários de serviços públicos desconcentrados, de prestadores de serviços, de empresários, de sindicatos, do meio universitário e de outros profissionais. Fez-se um esforço para recrutar mulheres, jovens e reformados, bem como pessoas que se supusesse terem pontos de vista alternativos no debate da regionalização. Reuniram-se 21 pessoas por cidade, e no total, participaram 83 pessoas. De entre estes participantes, obteve-se a representatividade desejada, com excepção de não ter sido possível recrutar mulheres e reformados na proporção planeada.

O formato, condução e análise dos Seminários foi da responsabilidade de uma equipa de 2 investigadores da RAND Europe e 5 correspondentes portugueses; estes últimos desempenharam as funções formais durante todas as sessões. A pessoa que dirigiu os seminários e a sua assistente têm experiência e conhecimento da legislação e do funcionamento do governo e da administração pública. Os três relatores das equipas são jovens professores universitários (Direito, Relações Internacionais e Ciência Política) também com experiência de administração publica. Antes e depois dos Seminários, a equipa beneficiou das opiniões do Conselho Consultivo do Projecto, que reúne personalidades do mundo político e académico, bem como do conselho da Fundação Luso Americana para o Desenvolvimento.

Cenários

Os cenários desenhados dividiam-se em dois grupos, designados por Quadros Gerais (cenários externos) e Quadros Específicos (cenários de descentralização). Foram construídas duas versões do Quadro Geral, uma apresentando um futuro de prosperidade para Portugal e a Europa, e outra pintando um quadro de crise económica. As sessões de Lisboa e Viseu foram realizadas sobre o quadro de prosperidade, enquanto as de Évora e Porto trabalharam o contexto de crise.

Os Quadros Específicos apresentavam três versões diferentes de descentralização

1) um voto sim no referendo, que levava à aplicação das leis 56/91 e 19/98;

2) um voto não no referendo, levando à devolução de competências do Governo central para os Municípios; e

3) cancelamento do referendo e instituição de centros regionais para tomada de decisão coordenada, dirigidos por elementos nomeados pelos Municípios.

Quadros Gerais. Os dois quadros gerais apresentavam uma imagem de Portugal e da Europa, em 2010, gozando de um prolongado período de crescimento económico, ou sofrendo a "Euro-depressão de 2007". Esta imagem foi dada através de:

- informação geral sobre o funcionamento da União Europeia e União Económica e Monetária e sobre o relacionamento de Portugal com a União Europeia;

- a situação económica em Portugal;

- a situação demográfica em Portugal;

- desenvolvimentos em áreas de maior importância, como saúde, segurança social, educação, ambiente, telecomunicações e habitação.

Cenários de descentralização. Os três cenários de descentralização, representavam três maneiras diferentes de reduzir o grau de centralização da Administração Pública em Portugal. Em cada Seminário, os participantes foram divididos por três equipas e cada equipa tratou um cenário diferente de descentralização. As equipas foram constituídas de modo a terem uma composição idêntica, incluindo em cada uma elementos das várias categorias definidas para recrutamento. Cada cenário começava com uma referência ao planeado referendo da regionalização, e depois descrevia em termos gerais as consequências e a forma como as 12 áreas de atribuição de competências especificadas na Lei 56/91, mais uma 13ª, a Saúde, eram geridas. Em cada um dos três cenários, era afirmado que a aplicação das decisões sobre descentralização era levada a cabo de boa fé, de modo a providenciar uma administração publica tão eficiente e eficaz e atenta às necessidades do público quanto possível.

Cenário A: "Sim" no referendo. Este cenário seguia de muito perto os termos da Lei 56/91. A pormenorização das atribuições foi retirada de descrições publicadas na imprensa portuguesa por partidários da regionalização.

Cenário B: "Não" no referendo . Este cenário partia do princípio que a derrota no referendo desacreditava a ideia das regiões. Em seu lugar, o governo central transferia muitas competências para as Câmaras. Embora não existissem formalmente órgãos de administração regional, os municípios auto organizavam-se, caso a caso, para melhor coordenação de esforços.

Cenário C - Cancelamento do Referendo. Este cenário tentava apresentar uma alternativa que proporcionasse alguma autonomia regional, mas sem a estrutura específica da lei 56/91 ou as 8 regiões da lei 19/98. Neste cenário eram criados 7 Centros de Decisão Regional, representando as duas Áreas Metropolitanas de Lisboa e do Porto mais as actuais cinco Comissões de Coordenação Regional, que actualmente funcionam como áreas de referência nos programas económicos e sociais da União Europeia. Em lugar do mecanismo da Assembleia Regional, os membros dos Centros de Decisão Regional eram eleitos pelos municípios, numa capacidade proporcional à respectiva população. As competências nas 12 áreas previstas na Lei 56/91, e na saúde, eram transferidas do governo central para esses órgãos, mas numa proporção menor e menos clara que no Cenário A. As delegações regionais dos Ministérios eram substituídas pelos Centros de Decisão Regional nas 7 cidades envolvidas (Lisboa, Porto e 5 sedes das CCR).

Actividades

Um dia num Seminário . Cada Seminário durou um dia inteiro, das 09.00h às 18.00h. Primeiro, apresentando-se o Quadro Geral de Portugal em 30 de Abril de 2010 a todo o grupo, após o que os participantes se dividiam em três equipas, cada qual com um cenário de descentralização diferente. Na companhia de um Relator, e seguindo uma série de perguntas que lhes eram entregues, os participantes discutiam o cenário durante 5 horas, com intervalo para o almoço. A concluir o dia, os participantes voltavam a reunir-se em conjunto, sendo-lhes pedido que comparassem as respectivas experiências no contexto dos diferentes cenários de descentralização e que discutissem algumas questões gerais.

Tarefas das equipas. O principal trabalho das equipas consistia em discutir os respectivos cenários com vista a responder a uma série de perguntas específicas. As três equipas recebiam um questionário idêntico, que se subdividia em quatro grupos de perguntas:

- Grupo 1 - Natureza dos financiamentos do governo e sua distribuição pelos diferentes níveis de poder local.

- Grupo 2 - Principais características do funcionamento da administração pública em Portugal, incluindo o grau de burocratização e regulamentação; a capacidade de resposta da Administração às necessidades dos cidadãos; acesso dos cidadãos aos serviços necessários; a coordenação dentro da Administração; a complexidade da formulação e execução de políticas públicas.

- Grupo 3 - A forma como a Administração irá lidar com sectores específicos , sendo as áreas submetidas a debate: educação, ambiente, saúde e catástrofes nacionais.

- Grupo 4 - Os pontos fortes e as deficiências do cenário do ponto de vista de diferentes grupos de interesses, como PME, grandes firmas industriais, reformados, etc.

Embora se pretendesse que todas as questões fossem debatidas, os debates focaram essencialmente os primeiros dois grupos de questões.

Sessão final

Na sessão final, os Relatores informavam todos os participantes sobre as características dos diferentes cenários, após o que se realizava uma discussão comparativa da experiência das três equipas , nomeadamente sobre:

- o funcionamento da Administração Publica (na sequência das perguntas do grupo 2);

- as qualificações necessárias aos funcionários públicos para assegurar uma descentralização eficaz ;

- questões relativas à coordenação com a União Europeia;

- áreas em que as competências deveriam permanecer centralizadas e áreas em que as competências deveriam ser descentralizadas.

RESULTADOS

Dos registos das discussões dos quatro Seminários, identificaram-se 9 temas principais. Alguns dos temas representam questões levantadas, senão em todas, na maior parte das equipas; outros temas assumiram diferente natureza ou relevância consoante os cenários ou locais de realização dos Seminários.

A - Efeito dos Quadros Gerais
B - Aceitação dos cenários de descentralização
C - A importância da descentralização
D - A melhor maneira de descentralizar
E - Distribuição e coordenação de responsabilidades
F - O Governo central como centro de gravidade da colecta e distribuição de recursos financeiros
G - A maneira adequada de distribuir recursos financeiros pelos diferentes níveis de poder
H - A distribuição de recursos humanos pelos diferentes níveis de poder
I - A solidariedade nacional

A - Efeito dos Quadros Gerais

Os Quadros Gerais foram apresentados aos participantes como uma situação plausível de Portugal em 2010, e a aceitação foi geral . Dito isto, não se verificou grande diferença entre os Seminários realizados sobre a hipótese de prosperidade e os que consideraram a "Euro-depressão". As equipas confrontadas com a depressão económica deliberaram numa atmosfera ligeiramente mais carregada - não havia grande disponibilidade de recursos para resolver problemas ou encontrar compromissos entre as diferentes posições assumidas pelos participantes. Por seu lado, as equipas que trabalharam na base da prosperidade económica apresentaram-se mais descontraídas, e menos preocupadas com as políticas. Sempre que possível, as dificuldades eram resolvidas gastando dinheiro.

B - Aceitação dos cenários de descentralização

Ao contrário dos cenários externos, registaram-se algumas objecções a alguns dos cenários de descentralização. Regra geral, as pessoas estavam preparadas para aceitar o Cenário A. Embora a ideia do Cenário B fosse também aceitável, houve algumas dificuldades em acatar a devolução de certas competências para os municípios. Não houve objecções ao cancelamento do referendo nem propriamente à ideia de Centros de Decisão Regional previstos no Cenário C, mas alguns participantes acharam que o cenário não era suficientemente específico para poder ser plenamente avaliado, e não compreenderam como iria funcionar.

Apesar de, em cada cenário, alguns elementos específicos (por exemplo, pormenores sobre competências) terem encontrado resistências aqui e ali, esses elementos variaram de sessão para sessão. No conjunto, é legítimo concluir que os cenários de descentralização foram aceites.

C - A importância da descentralização

Os participantes foram explícitos e praticamente unânimes na declaração de que é muito importante e muito necessária alguma forma de descentralização de competências. A presente organização da administração pública foi considerada excessivamente centralizada e já não capaz de lidar com os problemas da sociedade. Isto foi claro nos quatro Seminários e em todos os cenários de descentralização. Independentemente das preferências pessoais quanto à regionalização, a proposta apresentada no cenário era considerada preferível à opção de não haver descentralização.

Dito isto, os participantes fizeram notar também que, potencialmente, a descentralização terá lados negativos, que é preciso estar preparado para prevenir: poderão complicar-se a realização de mudanças estruturais e a formulação de políticas nacionais. Seria preferível que permanecessem centralizadas algumas políticas de implicação nacional (como relações externas, qualidade do ar), ou as que se prendem com áreas que representam conflitos de interesses em Portugal.

D - A melhor maneira de descentralizar

Embora fosse nítida a existência de um consenso quanto à necessidade de se efectuar uma descentralização, não se verificou acordo entre os participantes sobre o procedimento a seguir. Nem durante as sessões das equipas, nem nas sessões finais, foi possível identificar qualquer espécie de consenso sobre se o cenário A (voto sim) ou Cenário B (voto não) era a melhor escolha. O cenário C (Centros de Decisão Regional) não foi tão bem recebido como os outros porque os participantes não identificavam uma estrutura clara no cenário e, consequentemente, era-lhes difícil perspectivar os benefícios.

Quando os participantes manifestaram preferência pelas regiões administrativas (Cenário A), a razão mais citada foi a eficiência resultante da regionalização de competências. Quando os participantes se manifestaram a favor da devolução (Cenário B), a razão mais citada foi o facto de as Câmaras Municipais e as Freguesias saberem melhor o que as pessoas querem. Mas, mais importante que qualquer destas duas posições foi o consenso registado sobre 1) a necessidade de clarificar a maneira como poderá ser posta em pratica a regionalização; e 2) que no debate sobre o referendo faltava essa clarificação .

E - Distribuição e coordenação de responsabilidades

Os participantes focaram a necessidade de coordenação das políticas da Administração e houve consenso quanto a considerar uma definição clara das responsabilidades como condição importante para uma coordenação eficiente e eficaz. Os participantes também consideraram que esta definição clara não existia, nem dentro do Seminário, nem na mais vasta discussão pública sobre a qual se baseava o exercício em que estavam envolvidos.

Embora a discussão pública sobre a articulação entre o Governo e o poder local (no contexto da regionalização) incida principalmente na coordenação vertical (do central para o local, eventualmente para as regiões), os participantes também referiram a necessidade de coordenação horizontal - entre regiões ou entre municípios. No debate do referendo, nenhum dos lados parece interessar-se pela coordenação horizontal; e nos Seminários, no contexto do Cenário C, cuja principal característica era esse tipo de coordenação, a informação providenciada não foi julgada suficientemente específica. Os participantes consideraram que, em cada competência/atribuição susceptível de ser transferida, será preciso estudar cuidadosamente a coordenação horizontal. Em geral, quanto mais descentralizada for a competência, mais importante será a coordenação horizontal.

Os participantes também manifestaram a convicção de que o Governo central poderia ganhar em eficiência, eficácia e qualidade se (independentemente da regionalização) vários serviços fossem privatizados. Foi considerado importante determinar quais as tarefas da Administração Pública que poderiam ser mais bem desempenhadas por entidades privadas.

F - O Governo central como centro de gravidade da colecta e distribuição de recursos financeiros

Um aspecto óbvio - mas importante - levantado pelos participantes é que uma transferência substancial dos dinheiros públicos para o poder local (para as eventuais Regiões, Câmaras Municipais e Freguesias) é uma pré-condição para uma verdadeira descentralização . Registou-se consenso nos três cenários quanto à necessidade de haver uma fórmula determinada a nível nacional que estabeleça quanto dinheiro deve receber cada estrutura do poder local. Tal aumento de capacidade financeira deveria resultar da afectação de mais dinheiro do nível nacional para os níveis sub-nacionais da administração, e não de uma autorização aos poderes regional e/ou local para levantarem os seus próprios dinheiros.

G - Qual a maneira mais adequada de distribuir recursos financeiros pelos diferentes níveis de poder

Embora os participantes não especificassem uma fórmula nacional para a afectação dos recursos financeiros, houve acordo que uma tal fórmula deveria existir e que deveria conter mecanismos correctores dos desequilíbrios regionais.

A qualidade de um determinado modelo de descentralização depende em larga medida da forma como o poder local vai ser financiado. Isto quer dizer que uma proposta de descentralização apresentada ao país precisa de incluir alguma ideia sobre como será determinada essa fórmula nacional, e quais poderão ser as regras de funcionamento da autonomia.

H - A distribuição de recursos humanos pelos diferentes níveis de poder

Os participantes manifestaram a opinião que a qualidade das políticas da administração pública depende essencialmente da qualidade das pessoas que as vão executar. Ao pensar sobre a descentralização, é importante considerar que tipos de pessoal são necessários a todos os níveis da Administração pública e se este pessoal está disponível. Até agora, o tópico não recebeu grande atenção.

I - Solidariedade Nacional

Os participantes manifestaram-se claramente no sentido de que a regionalização não deveria levar a um aumento de diferenças entre ou intra regiões. Manifestaram algum medo que as diferenças entre as regiões pudessem aumentar em certas áreas como, por exemplo, estatuto sócio económico e acesso a cuidados de saúde. Deveriam ser criados mecanismos para garantir a solidariedade nacional e a coesão. Se a regionalização se concretizar, então o Governo central terá um papel importante na monitorização dos seus efeitos, e deveria actuar para mitigar desigualdades e injustiças que possam ocorrer.

IMPLICAÇÕES PARA O DEBATE DA REGIONALIZAÇÃO

O principal objectivo do exercício de prospectiva aqui relatado é informar o debate que rodeia o próximo referendo sobre a regionalização. Deste ponto de vista, talvez a conclusão mais importante seja a observação repetidamente feita pelos participantes de que é necessário melhorar a informação disponível com respeito à matéria para decisão do referendo.

Um número de participantes criticou o governo e o principal partido da oposição por má gestão do processo do referendo. Estes críticos declararam que ainda não houve um debate sério sobre a regionalização, e que o público ainda não recebeu suficiente informação para fazer uma escolha esclarecida. Estes e outros participantes indicaram que não percebiam bem qual era a proposta sobre que teriam de se pronunciar. Se cidadãos motivados e informados pensam desta forma, então não é certo que o eleitor médio, mesmo tentando informar-se, saiba por que está a votar. Uma consequência possível é uma alta taxa de abstenção.

Regionalização, Sim ou Não?

Uma das principais conclusões do nosso estudo é que todos pareciam ser a favor da descentralização. Não houve porém consenso sobre se a descentralização deve ser realizada pela aplicação da proposta de criação de Regiões que vai com o referendo (Cenário A), maior devolução de competências aos municípios (Cenário B) ou Centros de Decisão Regional coordenados numa base horizontal (Cenário C). Antes de decidir sobre a melhor maneira de descentralizar terão de ser claros os objectivos que se pretendem atingir com o processo de descentralização. Subsequentemente, poderá ser escolhido o modelo mais capaz de contribuir para alcançar tais objectivos.

Neste contexto, há que ver a questão do nível da descentralização. A maior parte das administrações públicas estão estruturadas em vários níveis, para os quais podem ser transferidas responsabilidades, ou seja, as responsabilidades de governo podem ser transferidas de maneiras diferentes.

Em Portugal, uma primeira opção é transferir poderes do nível nacional para o nível municipal existente (como no Cenário B). Uma segunda opção será transferir poderes do governo nacional para um dos níveis intermediários de administração , i.e. reforçar as entidades existentes entre o nível nacional e o local. Isto corresponderia a investir poder nos actuais 18 Distritos ou nas actuais cinco CCRs (ou ainda à respectiva modificação tal como apresentada no Cenário C). Uma terceira opção é criar um novo nível de poder local, para o qual podem ser transferidas responsabilidades , como no Cenário A. Até à data, tem sido esta a questão central no debate da regionalização em Portugal.

Os Seminários indicam que esta questão poderá não ser tão crítica quanto muitos acreditam, no sentido de que há várias maneiras possíveis de aplicar modelos diferentes de descentralização. O referendo está focado apenas numa forma específica de descentralização, a prevista nas Leis 56/91 e 19/98. Os pormenores dessa fórmula específica, incluindo o número e localização das Regiões e a instituição de uma Assembleia Regional eleita directamente, não deixam perceber pontos essenciais como seja a questão do funcionamento de qualquer órgão administrativo regional, ou de como esse órgão irá exercer as suas competências e interagir tanto com o governo central como com os municípios seus constituintes.

Informar o eleitorado

A nossa resposta à pergunta sobre regionalização na subsecção acima é "depende". A seguir indicamos as cláusulas de dependência.

O problema está nos detalhes - Os Seminários tornaram claro que os meios e os métodos de aplicação de qualquer modelo de descentralização são pelo menos tão importantes quanto as características específicas do modelo propriamente dito. O plano da regionalização vingará ou não conforme se processar a respectiva aplicação. Como o público será chamado a dar a sua opinião sobre a proposta específica prevista nas Leis 56/91 e 19/98 e não sobre uma pergunta abstracta sobre uma forma qualquer de administração regional, os pormenores de aplicação e execução prática **têm de ser** adiantados para esclarecer o voto. Os defensores do modelo proposto a referendo deveriam tornar claro quais os passos que vão ser tomados e em que lapso de tempo. O calendário para a devolução de competências e os planos de coordenação vertical e horizontal devem ser tornados explícitos; e pormenorizada a estrutura financeira em que se apoia o modelo.

O dinheiro conta muito - um dos pormenores que não tem sido discutido no presente debate da regionalização é como será financiada a nova estrutura de poder local . Os nossos participantes consideraram que não deveria ser alterada a estrutura financeira dos impostos nacionais e que deveria haver uma fórmula nacional para determinar a fatia de cada unidade de poder local . Além disso, houve acordo sobre a necessidade de pôr mais dinheiro à disposição do poder local. Enquanto os pormenores da formula nacional (plano de distribuição) não precisam de fazer parte do debate do referendo, seria vantajoso dar atenção aos montantes a disponibilizar para a administração regional (e, por seu turno, para os municípios e freguesias) e à autonomia de que disporão as administrações regionais para gastar esse dinheiro. Estamos em crer que o debate beneficiaria se fosse adiantada a filosofia em que se apoiaria a elaboração de uma fórmula nacional para regular a afectação de recursos. Esta filosofia deveria explicitar qual o entendimento da equidade, quais expectativas dirigidas às regiões mais ricas e mais pobres, qual a consideração a dar a necessidades específicas e como seriam feitos os ajustamentos exigidos por boas ou más conjunturas económicas.

As competências importam - Existem ambiguidades no plano de regionalização proposto no referendo não só no que respeita à afectação de recursos financeiros, mas também quanto à forma como as competências seriam transferidas. Aqui, é importante a forma de devolução. A descentralização de uma responsabilidade específica para um nível específico de poder local pode assumir muitas formas. A distinção mais importante é saber se as responsabilidades estão completamente descentralizadas (autonomia) ou são partilhadas entre diferentes níveis de poder (responsabilidades partilhadas). Quando se consideram as funções de uma administração regional, a diferença precisa de ser explicitada. O eleitorado seria bem servido por mais informação sobre a forma como as competências poderiam ser transferidas para as regiões, incluindo uma visão geral dos mecanismos de coordenação para as diferentes competências, um plano para a distribuição de recursos humanos e financeiros e uma consideração de mecanismos para corrigir as assimetrias susceptíveis de resultar da regionalização.

Para além do referendo.

Embora haja um forte movimento no sentido de descentralizar, é necessário acautelar que a descentralização - seja pela regionalização, seja por outros meios - não terá automaticamente efeitos positivos. É necessário reunir certas condições para que a descentralização vingue. Estas condições (como por exemplo, uma clara divisão de responsabilidades, uma clara distribuição de recursos humanos e financeiros e a coesão nacional) foram discutidas acima.

Seja qual for o resultado do referendo, e seja qual for o modelo de descentralização adoptado por Portugal, convém instituir um sistema de avaliação dos efeitos da descentralização. É praticamente certo que a aplicação não será perfeita - que algumas coisas vão funcionar bem e outras não tão bem. Pode acontecer que a descentralização tenha as consequências desejadas, e que mesmo assim, tenha resultados negativos (previstos ou imprevistos). Deveriam ser instituídos mecanismos para evitar ou mitigar quaisquer efeitos negativos directos ou laterais. Um sistema de avaliação, orientado para objectivos explícitos, permitirá a monitorização das mudanças e a adaptação e ajustamento do plano . Se se verificar que a regionalização na verdade permite atingir os objectivos definidos, serão dados novos passos nesse caminho. Se alguns (ou todos) os objectivos não forem atingidos, talvez seja necessário considerar formas alternativas de descentralização para certas competências. Se se assumir uma abordagem atenta e flexível Portugal estará em posição de garantir que a descentralização se realizará de maneira ordenada e eficiente.

ACKNOWLEDGMENTS

This research could not have been conducted without the cooperation of the people we interviewed and seminar game participants. These more than 100 people all gave generously of their time and knowledge. They are listed in Appendix A of the companion volume, but we wish here to give them our heartfelt thanks.

We thank RAND Europe colleagues Jonathan Cave, Lisa van Dorp, Rick Fallon and Robbin te Velde for assistance in the preparation of scenario materials. We also thank Michael Baum (Department of Political Science and Center for Portuguese Studies and Culture, University of Massachusetts-Dartmouth Campus) and RAND Europe colleague Erik Frinking for valuable and constructive criticism of an earlier draft of the manuscript.

We thank Rui Chancerelle de Machete, President of the Executive Council of the Luso-American Foundation for Development ("FLAD" for its Portuguese name) for his advice and assistance in all phases of this project. We also thank FLAD Executive Council member Bernardino Gomes and the members of the project Advisory Board—João Caupers, Leonardo Ferraz de Carvalho, Carlos Gaspar, Luís Valente de Oliveira and António Vitorino—for their wise counsel at crucial steps of the work.

Finally, the RAND Europe authors thank the warm and friendly staff of FLAD for their assistance in helping visitors to Portugal find their way—logistically, geographically and bureaucratically.

CHAPTER 1: INTRODUCTION

REGIONALIZATION IN PORTUGAL

The Portuguese Constitution of 1976 defined a national and local level of government. On the national level, governance is through the interplay of three central actors: the President of the Republic (elected directly), the *Assembleia da República* ("National Assembly," also elected directly) and the *Conselho de Ministros* ("Council of Ministers," commonly referred to as "the Government"). The head of the Government is the Prime Minister, who is appointed by the President after consultation with the National Assembly. The other ministers are appointed by the President on the proposal of the Prime Minister. On the local level, the constitution makes provision for three levels of representation, *freguesias* ("parishes," corresponding more or less to "wards" or "councils" in the Anglo-American world), *municípios* (almost always translated "municipalities" but actually corresponding more to American counties) and *regiões administrativas* ("administrative regions").[1] The two lowest levels are a continuation of well-established governmental bodies in Portugal; the difference is that since the post-revolutionary constitution of 1976, the 4241 parishes and 306 municipalities are governed by directly elected representative bodies.

The administrative regions, on the other hand, have not yet been implemented, and the constitution does not specify the powers and competencies they should possess. Portugal has five Central Coordinating Regions (CCRs) for socio-economic planning, but these are implementation units of the national government with advisory powers and their members are not locally elected or appointed.[2] Mainland Portugal also has 18 *distritos administrativos* ("administrative districts") that serve to define electoral units for proportional representation in national elections; as administrative centers for police, courts, and other public order functions; and as the basis for siting some (but far from all) local offices of ministries. Although each district has a *Governador Civil* ("civil governor") for matters concerning public order—nominated by the *Ministro da Administração Interna* ("Minister of Home Affairs") and appointed by the Government, there is no locally appointed or chosen governance at the district level. Hence,

---

[1] The two offshore areas of Portugal—the islands of the Azores and Madeira—are autonomous regions, with their own elected legislative bodies and considerable local powers. The autonomy of these islands is dictated by their considerable distance from mainland Europe and tradition. As there is no talk of creating regional legislative bodies—much less giving such autonomous power to any mainland regional government—we shall not discuss regional autonomy or the situation of the Azores and Madeira further in this report.
[2] The CCRs are used by the European Union for purposes of regional development and planning.

administrative <u>districts</u> are not administrative <u>regions</u> in the sense of the Portuguese Constitution.

Current thought in Portugal with respect to regional governance goes back to the 1950s and 1960s.[3] Between 1976 and 1991, the debate on regionalization was sporadic, with the political parties wavering between traditional centralism and moderate decentralization.[4] With Portugal's entry into the European Union (EU), however, pressures for regionalization increased, in keeping with a general principal of subsidiarity, or devolving government functions to as local a level as possible.

Regionalization in Portugal is made difficult because there are, with the exception of the Algarve at the southern tip of the country, few historically or culturally legitimate "natural" mainland regional boundaries. The country's national boundaries have been in place longer than any other European country, and the Portuguese are a remarkably homogeneous people with respect to social characteristics such as language, race and religion. Although there are geographical areas within the country that—by culture, economic base, geological terrain or demography—have a well-established identity, there is not a consensus that these areas would be the clear choice in defining administrative regions. Thus the proposed referendum on regionalization has included a specification of how many regions there would be and where regional boundaries would be drawn; these have become part of the debate, sometimes clouding the larger issues.

A major watershed in the regionalization debate occurred in August 1991, when the National Assembly passed Law 56/91, detailing a method of choosing *assembleias regionais* ("regional assemblies") and *juntas* (regional executive organs) in mainland Portugal. This law did not create these bodies, but only set out a specification to be offered to the Portuguese population in a referendum. It specified that the regional assemblies would be elected partly by direct vote[5] and partly by appointment from municipalities. Regional assemblies would have no legislative power, but would appoint the regional executive organs and approve the actions of the executive.

Law 56/91 also specified a set of competencies the regional administrative bodies would exercise, in taking on responsibilities presently belonging to the central government. It did not, however, determine how the regional administrations and central government would coordinate their respective powers, or which specific tasks would devolve to the

---

[3] Portugal was under a dictatorship from 1928 until 1974. Although this regime was highly centralized, it considered (but never implemented) administrative regions.
[4] Pinto, A.C., *Modern Portugal,* 1998, p. 216.
[5] The regional assembly direct vote would follow the general plan of all elections in Portugal where party slates obtain proportional seating.

regions. The regions as contemplated would follow the general philosophy of the French regions in that they would have no legislative powers and have a primary responsibility for economic and social development. Their most important task would be to plan regional development. They would deal with urban policy in a general way, but take no power from the current municipalities; some services would be transferred from central national ministries to the regions, but nothing would be transferred upwards from municipalities. Criminal justice matters would remain within the competency of the national government. In general, interests of the region would prevail in decision-making except for "central national services."

Law 56/91 thus developed a structure for regional administration and provided the main reference point for subsequent regionalization discussions. It did not, however, provide a map to identify how many regions there would be or their boundaries. Following the passage of the law, the regionalization issue arose in the electoral campaigns preceding the October 1995 general elections and the January 1996 presidential election. However, the debate did not focus on party lines; leaders of most major parties were to be found on either side of the issue.

The next major act regarding regionalization was the passage in October 1997 by the National Assembly of Decree 190/VII, which became Law 19/98 in April 1998. This law drew a map of eight administrative regions for implementing Law 56/91. The eight suggested regions largely split the country along north-south lines (following the current CCRs), but also separate littoral from interior areas in the north of the country. Municipalities would not be split by a regional boundary; indeed, only one of the current 18 administrative districts (Lisboa/Setúbal) would be distributed between two different regions.

Since the passage of the decree, the debate on regionalization has increased in intensity, if not clarity. The non-partisan aspect of the regionalization debate weakened, and the votes for Law 19/98 largely followed party lines, with the PS (Socialist Party) favoring and PSD (Social Democratic Party) opposing holding the referendum. Parties to the left of the PS are generally in favor of regionalization, but parties to the right of the PSD are not necessarily opposed to it.

On 1 September 1998, the *Diário da República* published Decree 39/98, whereby the President of the Republic set a date of 8 November 1998 for a referendum on regionalization.[6,7] This referendum is to consist of the following two questions:

1. Do you agree with the concrete plan to institute administrative regions?
2. Do you agree with the concrete plan to institute an administrative region in the area where you vote?

The "concrete plan" in the first question has been interpreted by the Portuguese Constitutional Court to refer to Law 56/91, and the introductory text to the second labels its "concrete plan" as the list of regions in Law 19/98.

A REFERENDUM ON WHAT?

There is a significant question in the minds of many Portuguese voters of what the change in governance brought about by the referendum would mean. As the matter is debated, it is clear that the issue is not decentralization of government. In almost all positions with respect to the referendum, there is a recognition of the need for the modernization of the State, meaning a more active role for citizenship and for the values and practices associated with it, in keeping with public opinion, which is increasingly vocal in its demands. This modernization is also seen by almost all parties as requiring a decentralization of government. The debate is about the best way to achieve decentralization.

There is also a consensus that decentralization must be accompanied by a transfer of tax revenues from the national to some form of local government[8] (although there are few precise formulas suggested to date), and there is a consensus that a decentralization policy should include transfers from richer to poorer areas of the country to further economic equality (again, with few specifics discussed).

The debate, then, is about whether regionalization is the best way to achieve decentralization, and if so, what form regionalization should take. However, this debate is

---

[6] The Portuguese constitution provides strict guidelines for both the timing and wording of referenda. A national referendum is a distinct ballot, separated in time from national elections or other referenda. The language must be simple and the issue presented clear-cut; the meaning of a "yes" or "no" vote must be obvious to the voter. In order for the result to be binding, half of the eligible electorate must vote. It is interesting to note in this regard that only one national referendum has been previously held (28 June 1998 on liberalization of abortion), and the voter turnout of 32 percent was insufficient to validate the outcome.

[7] This paper presents a report of activities conducted in June 1998. At that time, neither the date nor the text of the referendum were known; indeed, both were the topic of considerable debate at the time.

[8] Local governments currently receive approximately eight percent of revenues; one of the lowest percentages in Europe and one-fifth the percentage of some other EU countries.

far from clear; arguments invoked in favor of or against regionalization often sound the same. For example, proponents claim that regionalization will result in more efficient government, as those responsible for policies will be closer to the delivery of services. They argue that efficiency is increased by having things close to home, that regional government offices located in an administrative center can serve for "one-stop shopping" instead of the current situation where people need to go to 3 or 4 places (each ministry can place its branch offices as it sees fit), and that regions can be responsive to needs of locals better than can Lisboa. Opponents, on the other hand, claim that regionalization will result in less efficient government, through the imposition of another layer of bureaucracy. These people argue that one more layer of government just introduces inefficiency and political opportunism, and that the municipalities, either singly or working together, are quite capable of handling local interests.

A SEMINAR GAME TO INFORM THE DEBATE

In this political environment—where the results of the policy choices at hand are unclear—the use of seminar gaming to explore the possibilities of different decentralization alternatives is attractive. A comparison of informed opinions of how Portugal might function under several proposed decentralization schemes might inform the referendum debate by providing a more concrete picture of the likely results of moving to one or another form of regional administrative governance or alternative means of decentralization. At the request of the *Fundação Luso-Americana para o Desenvolvimento* ("Luso-American Foundation for Development," commonly known as FLAD for the acronym of its Portuguese name), RAND Europe designed and conducted a series of such seminar games, which took place in four Portuguese cities (Lisboa, Évora, Viseu, and Porto) in June 1998. This paper is a report of that experience.

Chapter 2 of this paper describes the methodology of the RAND Europe project. After a short introduction on seminar gaming, we describe the overall design of the game, the characteristics of the participants in the four game sessions, the materials provided the participants, and the instructions governing the work the participants did during the course of the seminar games. Chapter 3 identifies nine important themes that arose during the seminar games and describes and discusses the results of the four sessions in terms of those themes. For each theme, there is a description of what has been said and what conclusions can be drawn from that information.[9] The fourth

---

[9] A companion volume, in Portuguese, presents the actual documents used to conduct the game, including scenario information provided the players and the instructions given the teams, as well as summaries of the deliberations that took place.

and last chapter builds on the third chapter. It provides implications of the seminar games for the regionalization debate, including what information is needed to further inform the electorate about the choices posed by the referendum, factors seen by the seminar game participants that might favor or not favor regionalization in the form of Laws 56/91 and 19/98, and recommendations for how to proceed once the results of the referendum are known.

CHAPTER 2: METHOD OF THE STUDY

This chapter discusses the method we used to understand different forms of decentralization in Portugal. We will give a short description of the methodology of seminar games and we will explain why we chose this method to provide input to the regionalization debate. Thereafter, we will describe our study method in terms of the three central characteristics of a seminar game: participants, scenario, and tasking.

SEMINAR GAMES: A SHORT INTRODUCTION

Seminar gaming is an approach to understanding complex problems that capitalizes on the inherent expertise of groups of participants. The central characteristics of a seminar game are:

- Participants perform in groups. The central task of a seminar game is a focused discussion on a complex topic. The interaction among the participants yields knowledge beyond the sum of the knowledge of the single participants.

- The discussion is centered around a specific situation, almost always cast into the future. Borrowing from theatre terminology, this situation is termed a *scenario*. Because the scenario is specific, the discussion is forced to be on the basis of specific characteristics, rather than being an abstract discussion of values or opinions. Because the scenario is set in the future, participants are detached from their beliefs on current specific issues.

- The group's discussion is further focused by specific questions regarding the scenario they must address or specific decisions in the context of the scenario they must make. These questions and decisions serve to bring out the variety of experiences, knowledge and opinions held by the participants, as they search for a common basis of understanding. Agreements and disagreements among the participants are revealed through these concrete tasks in a way that is more difficult when the discourse is in terms of abstract generalizations.

Thus, a seminar game is characterized by three central attributes: (1) the participants and how they are grouped into "teams," (2) the scenario that is presented, and (3) the tasks the teams are asked to perform.

Seminar gaming is an attractive research tool to study the social issue of regionalization for a number of reasons. First, the issue involves a great number of different actors, who are often intentionally or unintentionally operating at cross purposes. Different levels of government and various segments of the private sector have different organizational structures with different objectives and different strategic orientations. Bringing them together to consider different decentralization strategies increases mutual understanding and identifies what issues are affected by decentralization. Second, the available information regarding different forms of decentralization is incomplete and inconclusive. This means that seminar gaming provides a method to gain insights that are not obtainable by other means. Third, seminar gaming provides a "safe" environment in which participants may explore issues without having to face real-life consequences.

A seminar game can have different objectives. In general, a seminar game is not aimed at solving a problem, but at better understanding a problem. By allowing interaction among different actors with different backgrounds, experiences, and responsibilities, seminar gaming makes it possible to better understand a problem. The interaction encourages the analysis of the situation from several points of view, as well as the exchange of ideas. Such an interaction can lead to results that never could have been arrived at had the interaction not taken place. A game draws people into an ongoing discussion in an active and creative way.

Why a seminar game on regionalization?

Regionalization in Portugal is a complicated, politically charged, but often vaguely understood issue. Many different interests play a role in the discussion on regionalization. Therefore, we believed that seminar gaming—that is addressing regionalization by examining how different forms of decentralized administrative government might work under various possible futures—could help clarify and inform the public debate in Portugal. In this seminar game, specific competencies that have been proposed for decentralization have been assessed in the light of different possible socio-economic futures, under different types of decentralized administration, to be considered by participants from four different geographical areas of the country.

OVERVIEW OF THE GAME DESIGN

We conducted four seminar game sessions on four different days: 16, 19, 23 and 25 June 1998. The games were played in four different cities: Lisboa, Évora, Viseu and Porto, respectively. Thus, we involved people from one larger and one smaller city in the southern part of Portugal and one larger and one smaller city in the northern part of the country. In this way, we were able, via comparing results, to better understand differences in attitudes towards administrative regions that might depend on urban vs. rural areas and north vs. south.

Information collected as an input to the seminar game

To prepare for the seminar game, we conducted interviews and a literature study. These activities were aimed at identifying topics that are relevant to the future functioning of the Portuguese government. The information was used to guide participant selection, to design the scenario materials, and to determine what tasks to assign the participants.

Interviews were with government officials, university professors, and other experts. The interviews totaled about twenty people, and all took place in Lisboa; names of the interviewees are listed in Appendix A. The interviewees were asked what they believed would be the most important consequences of regionalization in Portugal, with particular emphasis on how it might affect their particular area of expertise. In this way, a list of relevant topics was created.

Our desk research included both books and internet web sites, and was designed to acquire statistical and other information to be used in scenario design. A list of resources consulted may be found at the end of this volume.

A day at a seminar game

Each game lasted an entire day, beginning at about 9:00 and lasting until after 18:00. The game began with an introduction, which provided (1) an opportunity for the participants to meet the game organizers and each other, (2) information about games in general and the reason, purpose and scope of the day's events, and (3) the schedule for the day. This introduction was followed by a presentation of a possible future for Portugal on 30 April 2010. This future, which we term the "external scenario," will be elaborated upon below. The presentation took about 30 minutes.

Following an opportunity for questions regarding the external scenario, the participants were divided into three teams and, following a short break, adjourned to separate rooms to receive more information. In these separate rooms, participants were told what particular form of governmental decentralization had taken place in Portugal between 1998 and 2010; these forms of government make up the "decentralization scenario" below. Further, the participants were presented with a set of specific questions (the "tasking") to answer as they discussed the world they had been presented. Each team within a city was thus given a different version of the decentralization scenario to consider in light of the one external scenario that had been presented to the entire group of participants meeting in a city.

The teams then engaged in discussion for a total of four to five hours, interrupted by a lunch lasting about two hours.[10] After this discussion, the entire group reassembled for about 45 minutes to summarize their separate deliberations and to answer some general questions.

PARTICIPANTS IN THE SEMINAR GAMES

There are a number of different roles played in a seminar game. A game is conducted by what in gaming parlance is called a "control team." The control team is led by a facilitator, or game director, whose task it is to create a pleasant atmosphere, to explain the objective of the game, to answer questions of the participants and to stimulate interaction among participants. The other members of the control team consisted of two RAND Europe staff to ensure that the overall design was followed and assist the game director, an assistant director to oversee the logistics of the game, and three "rapporteurs" to chair each team as it performed its independent work.

The control team and Advisory Board

The game director was a Portuguese woman with considerable experience in Portuguese government, the diplomatic service, and as a private consultant. The assistant director was a Portuguese employee of FLAD who has a background in legal studies. The three rapporteurs were Portuguese junior university professors in law, international relations and economics; they also have experience in government. The two RAND Europe staff were an American social psychologist with extensive experience in the design and conduct of seminar games and a Dutch researcher with training in public administration who has been involved in seminar gaming in the Netherlands.

A project Advisory Board of senior Portuguese former government officials, academics and consultants met with the control team at various times to constructively criticize the seminar game design, offer advice and assistance on participant selection and critique a preliminary draft of this manuscript. The members of the Advisory Board are named in Appendix A of the companion volume.

Participant recruitment

After defining what kind of participants would be most valuable in playing the game (mid-level people from different professional backgrounds), different people (rapporteurs, members of the advisory board, spokesmen for different organizations) were approached

---

[10] All participants had lunch together. In order not to have teams influence each other, participants were cautioned not to discuss seminar game matters during their lunch break.

to propose participants for the game.[11] These candidates were then contacted by telephone to ascertain their interest and availability on the dates of the sessions. People willing to participate were sent a confirmation by mail or fax with information on time and location of the game. Finally, the person was called one day before the game for a last reminder.

In general, the people contacted were very interested in participating; it was not difficult to find adequate numbers of participants. The difficulty in recruitment was to ensure a balance among the participants with regard to professional background, gender,[12] age group and different opinions regarding regionalization.

Participant characteristics

For each game session, 21 people were invited to participate. They were recruited from elected officials, entrepreneurs, professionals, university-based people, labor union officials, civil servants and service providers. Some participants belonged to more than one group. In the table below, we list participants according to their primary affiliation. In total, then, 84 individuals (21 people for each of the four game sessions) were invited to participate and 83 actually attended. One person in Lisboa and one person in Porto had to cancel his attendance on one day's notice and informed us beforehand; we were able to find a last-minute substitute for the Lisboa absentee but not for the Porto one. It is noteworthy that there were not any "no-shows," i.e., persons who said they would come and then failed to attend. Table 1 summarizes the characteristics of the participants.[13]

The three teams within each city were composed by randomly assigning participants, subject to distributing them as equally as possible according to the categories shown in Table 1. We also informally attempted to ensure that each team would have participants who favored and participants who were opposed to regionalization.[14]

The participants were paid 50.000 escudos (about 250 euro) for their participation.[15] Candidates were not informed about this honorarium when recruited, but were told about it in the letter confirming their participation. The payment was made to partially

---

[11] We did not set out to recruit a set of participants representative of the Portuguese population as a whole; such an undertaking, even if possible, would have required an expenditure of effort, time and money beyond our resources. Instead, we attempted to balance our selection in ways that would avoid bias in how regionalization is perceived.

[12] Although every effort was made to recruit more women, only 16 women participated.

[13] The names of the participants may be found in Appendix A in the companion volume.

[14] Most participants did not have public positions in the regard. However, based on our conversations with the participants before and after the day's activities, we believe we were successful.

[15] This payment may have helped keep the participation rate high, but probably was rarely the determining factor in an individual's decision to attend.

compensate for the day's loss of work and to emphasize the importance of the project. Payment was made to the participants at the end of the day.

Table 1: Characteristics of Participants

Site:	Lisboa	Évora	Viseu	Porto	Total
Characteristic:					
Total participants	21	21	21	20	**83**
Demographics					
Women	5	4	3	4	**16**
Under age 30	2	4	3	4	**13**
Over age 49	4	2	2	4	**12**
Selection criterion					
Elected officials	3	3	3	3	**12**
Entrepreneurs	3	3	3	2	**11**
Professionals	6	6	6	6	**24**
University-based	3	3	3	3	**12**
Labor union officials	0	3	0	3	**6**
Civil servants	3	3	3	3	**12**
Service providers	3	0	3	0	**6**

SCENARIOS

The scenario is the principle tool of a seminar game. It removes the participants from their everyday lives and places them in the context of the game situation. In order to accomplish this, a scenario must have the following characteristics:

- It must be plausible, but it does not have to be probable. Indeed, given the uncertainty of the future, we explicitly state that the scenario is <u>not</u> a prediction, but only a possibility, as likely as many other possibilities.

- It must be internally consistent in order to be plausible and in order to enable a coherent discussion.

- It does not describe the developments that led to the described picture of the future. Instead, participants might be asked to project backwards from the posited future to better understand how that future might arise.[16]

- It contains enough information to describe the functioning of a decentralized Portuguese government in 2010.

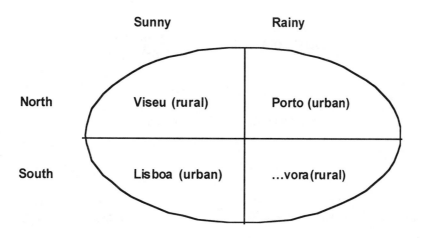

Figure 1: Game sessions

The scenario materials we designed can be divided into two groups, which we have termed the "external scenario" and the "decentralization scenario". Two different forms of the external scenario were constructed, termed the *cenario ensoleirado* ("sunny scenario") and *cenario chuvoso* ("rainy scenario"), respectively. All participants at any seminar game session were only shown one of the external scenarios; this was "their" future and the existence of other possible futures was not discussed.[17] The seminar game sessions in Lisboa and Viseu employed the sunny scenario while the seminar game sessions in Évora and Porto employed the rainy scenario. Thus, one game session in the north and one game session in the south received each external scenario, while one game session in an urban area and one game session in a rural area received each external scenario. This is shown in Figure 1.

---

[16] In the jargon of futurology and gaming, our technique is called "backcasting" to distinguish it from the more familiar forecasting.

[17] Participants were not told of the name given their external scenario.

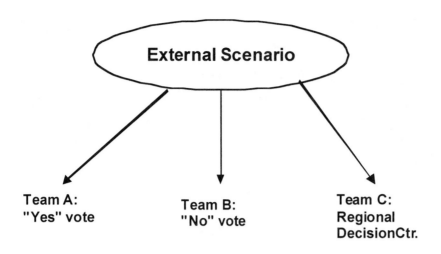

Figure 2: Decentralization scenarios

Three different forms of the decentralization scenario were constructed, representing respectively (1) a "yes" vote in the proposed referendum on administrative regions, (2) a "no" vote in the proposed referendum, and (3) a different form of administrative regions following a cancellation of the proposed referendum. At each game session, every decentralization scenario was used, one scenario per team. Figure 2 shows this schematically.

External scenarios

The two external scenarios differed largely in the economic picture of Portugal (and the surrounding European Union). The materials used to present these scenarios are provided as Appendix B in the companion volume. In the sunny scenario, Europe in 2010 was enjoying a prolonged period of economic prosperity, while in the rainy scenario, the good times had come to an end with the "Euro-depression of 2007."[18] Within these two general frameworks, the scenarios were fleshed out by information on the following subjects:

- General information on the functioning of the European Union and the Economic and Monetary Union and on the relationship between Portugal and the European
- The economic situation in Portugal.
- The demographic situation in Portugal.

---

[18] Some elements of the external scenarios did not vary between the sunny and rainy versions, because the differences in the socio-economic situation do not necessarily lead to different developments in these areas.

- Developments in major policy areas. Information was provided on health care, social security, education, environment, infrastructure, telecommunications and housing.

The sunny scenario. This external scenario was designed to portray as positive a picture of Portugal and the EU as might realistically be expected. We portrayed an expanded EU that was increasingly economically and politically integrated, with a European Monetary Union that met or exceeded all expectations. Although Portugal's increased prosperity (buttressed by an average growth of 3,7 percent in the twelve years 1998-2010) was even greater than the EU average, it was still the recipient of support through the Structural Funds and the Cohesion Fund. The Portuguese economic engine was primarily driven by the service sector, although the industrial and agricultural sectors also contributed. Portugal was the beneficiary of increased internationalization of investment, which supported a strong decrease in unemployment.

The demographic and social situation was similarly sunny. Although the birth rate, which was below the substitution level in 1998, did not markedly increase, migration kept the population at a stable level. Urbanization continued to increase, but the migration from the interior to the coast slowed down as all areas of the country shared in the prosperity. Housing shortages had greatly decreased and slums were disappearing. Health care delivery had improved, but not as much as might be desired; Portugal was still near the bottom of Western European countries, and many inequities continued to exist. Supported by the general prosperity and helped by low unemployment, public welfare was extensive and affordable. Substantial improvements had been made in literacy and the number of Portuguese people obtaining higher education. With increased prosperity relieving economic worries, environmental issues were high on the political agenda, especially with regard to water and waste management. The physical and electronic infrastructure had been extensively developed; most works projected for the first decade of the 21st Century had been achieved.

The rainy scenario. This scenario was designed to provide a contrast to the sunny one, where economic prosperity was not available as a buffer between government and social problems. We posited that the general prosperous trend was interrupted in the year 2007 by a major Europe-wide depression, from which the continent was just beginning to recover. Although the European Monetary Union had not collapsed, most of the members regretted joining it, and nations joining the EU did not join the monetary union. European political integration had also suffered as a consequence. The twelve-year average economic growth in Portugal was 1,5 percent (a strong increase up to 2007 made the net growth positive), and the service sector had driven the previous growth. The EU

Structural and Cohesion Funds had shortages and foreign investment had fallen drastically, so Portugal could not call upon those funds to correct deficiencies. While the country suffered from the Euro-depression generally, Lisboa was less disadvantaged, because many of the service sector functions in the capital continued.

The general demographic and social scene in Portugal followed from the economic one. Unemployment rose from 6,7 percent to 9,0 percent, and was pervasive across both highly skilled and less-skilled people. The total population size fell, because migration by job seekers disappeared. Indeed, there was a net emigration as Portuguese left the country to seek work abroad. Trends towards urbanization did not stop, as people left the countryside for the cities in search of jobs; slums increased as these people did not find work. Health care delivery improved (but less than in the sunny scenario); waiting lists remained a serious problem. Social security was suffering, and the government incurred considerable debt providing public welfare. Although literacy had increased, the number of people obtaining higher education had not met expectations. Environmental issues were not high on the political agenda because of economic worries. Many planned infrastructures had been delayed or even cancelled for lack of funds.

Decentralization scenarios

There were three decentralization scenarios, representing three different ways of dealing with the perceived need to reduce the degree of centralization of Portuguese governance. Each scenario began with a reference to the planned regionalization referendum, went on to describe in general terms the subsequent consequences, and then described how the twelve competency areas for regions specified in Law 56/91 (plus health as an added area)[19] were managed:

- Economic and social development;
- Spatial planning;
- Environment, nature preservation and water management;
- Transport and communication infrastructure;
- Housing;
- Education and vocational training;
- Culture and national heritage;
- Youth, sports and leisure;
- Tourism;
- Public utilities;
- Agricultural support;
- Municipal support;
- Health.

---

[19] Although health is not included in Law 56/91, the decentralization of health care delivery policy has been a topic of considerable discussion.

Scenario A: "Yes" on the referendum. This decentralization scenario took Laws 56/91 and 19/98 as its starting point and followed the language of those documents and current newspaper stories describing plans for regional administration. The scenario began:

> In November 1998, after a twelve-day electoral campaign, a national referendum was held on whether or not to establish an elected regional level of government. The results were in favor of the pro-regionalization position. In fact, with the support of the majority of left and center-left parties, as well as some marginal center-right voters, the yes position has reached 53,3% of the expressed votes, against 46,7% for the no supporters. The abstention level was 24% of the registered voters. Following the referendum, there was a national spirit of putting the debate to rest and getting on with the job of installing a regional government.

As a consequence of this referendum, eight administrative regions were established in continental Portugal:[20]

> *Região de Entre Douro e Minho*
> *Região de Trás-os-Montes e Alto Douro*
> *Região da Beira Litoral*
> *Região da Beira Interior*
> *Região da Estremadura e Ribatejo*
> *Região de Lisboa e Setúbal*
> *Região do Alentejo*
> *Região do Algarve*

The method of election of the eight different regional assemblies and the selection of the regional administration followed Law 56/91.

The adoption of administrative regions led to two major changes in the administrative structure of the country. First, the newly created regions took over all tasks of the 5 CCRs. In addition, every region has a civil governor. Second, the regions have subsumed some of the central government's functions in the 13 areas of competency. As a consequence, ministerial administrative offices outside of the capital have been replaced by regional offices in the eight regional chief cities, while for the other competencies, ministerial offices were relocated to the eight regional chief cities. With the reorganization, there has been a net decrease of 10 percent in the total number of administrative offices, but no corresponding decrease in the number of personnel staffing these offices.

Scenario B: "No" on the referendum. This devolution scenario was intended to be the mirror image of Scenario A. However, as maintenance of the current centralized regime was viewed as unrealistic, we presented it as an alternative to administrative regions to achieve decentralization. The introductory paragraph read as follows:

---

[20] Maps showing the regions for Scenarios A and C can be found in Appendix C of the companion volume.

In November 1998, the Portuguese, consulted via a national referendum, rejected regionalization. After a twelve day electoral campaign, the no position has reached 53,3% of the expressed votes, and 46,7% of the voters supported regionalization. The abstention level was 24% of the registered voters. The debate surrounding the referendum made clear that the no vote was not a statement of support for a dominant central government, but rather a rejection of elected regional bodies as an alternative. Therefore following the referendum, there was a national spirit in favor of subsidiarity and considerable activity devolving many government functions from the national level to local government.

The form of decentralization chosen for this scenario was to move some competencies from the central government to municipalities and for others to make the local distribution of ministerial administration more efficient and responsive to government. We therefore posited the passage of a Law of Devolution which formed the basis for significant reforms. As a consequence, in many of the 13 competency areas of ministerial administrative offices outside of the capital were replaced by local offices, while for the other areas, ministerial offices were relocated and generally merged. Although there was no formal supra-municipal organizational structure, municipalities often harmonized policies when faced with common problems and ad hoc multi-municipality organizations were created. With the reorganization, there was a net decrease of 20 percent in the number of ministerial administrative offices, but, taking into account the additional resources required by local government, no corresponding decrease and perhaps a small increase in the number of personnel performing governmental functions.

Scenario C: Regional decision centers. This scenario was constructed on the principle that some form of regional governance might be a good idea, but the specific implementation plan of Laws 56/91 and 19/98, in terms of the eight named regions and an elected regional assembly, might be replaced by a different structure. The introductory text to this scenario read as follows:

> After much soul-searching, the PS and the PSD jointly announced in early October 1998 a decision that the planned referendum on elected regional administration would not be held. The debate in the preceding year had made clear that while there was clear support for some form of devolution of authority from the central authorities, the best way to accomplish that devolution was far from clear, and therefore a referendum on one form of regionalization was premature. Following this decision, there was a national spirit in favor of subsidiarity and considerable thought about how to devolve many government functions from the national level. This thinking culminated in a law of the creation of administrative regions and metropolitan areas which formed the basis for subsequent actions.

The law created seven "regional decision centers" as follows:

Centro de Decisão Regional de Lisboa
Centro de Decisão Regional do Porto
Centro de Decisão Regional do Norte
Centro de Decisão Regional do Centro
Centro de Decisão Regional do Vale do Tejo
Centro de Decisão Regional do Alentejo
Centro de Decisão Regional do Algarve

These were constructed by using the present five CCRs and separating out the two metropolitan areas of Lisboa and Porto to become independent decision centers.

The decision centers took over all tasks of the 5 CCRs and subsumed many of the central government's administrative competencies, especially in the 12 areas mentioned in Law 56/91, plus health. As a consequence, ministerial administrative offices outside of the capital were replaced by regional offices in the five regional chief cities plus Lisboa and Porto, while for the other competencies, ministerial offices (including police regional centers) were relocated to the regional chief cities. With the reorganization, there was a net decrease of 10 percent in the number of administrative offices, but no corresponding decrease in the number of personnel staffing these offices. Administrators for the decision centers were chosen by voting of the municipal assemblies in the center, where the vote of a municipality was weighted by its population size. To prevent domination, especially in the Lisboa and Porto decision centers, no municipality could have a weight larger than one-third.

TEAM TASKING AND CLOSING SESSION

The major work of the teams was to discuss their scenarios in order to answer specific questions posed to them. A common set of questions was used in all four cities for all three teams, broken into four question sets. The full text of the question sets and summary notes of the teams' responses to these questions are provided in Appendix C of the companion volume.

- **Question set 1:** The nature and allocation of government financing for different levels of government.

- **Question set 2:** Key characteristics of the functioning of the Portuguese government, including the degree of bureaucratization and regulation, the responsiveness of the government to the citizens' needs, access of citizens to the needed services, the need for coordination within the Portuguese government and the complexity of policy formulation and implementation.

- **Question set 3:** The way in which the government will deal with specific competencies; specific areas queried included education, environment, health care and disaster management.

- **Question set 4:** The strengths and weaknesses of the scenario from the viewpoint of different interest groups, such as small and medium enterprises, large industrial firms, unskilled and semi-skilled laborers, retirees and people desiring to preserve the Portuguese culture and national heritage.

At the beginning of each team meeting, the rapporteur asked one member of the team to write down the result of the team's deliberations. One team chose to shift this burden among different members for different question sets, but the rest of the teams had one "secretary."[21]

Although it was our intention to have all questions discussed, some teams spent considerable time answering the first two question sets, leaving little or no time for the third or fourth sets.

After the teams had completed their task, but no later than 17:30 in the afternoon, the participants were brought back together into one group for a closing session. In this closing session, the three different decentralization scenarios were revealed to all of the participants and summaries of each team's deliberations were made. The discussion followed a protocol aimed at gaining insight into comparisons among team results regarding:

- The functioning of the Portuguese government (largely following question set 2, above).
- The qualifications government personnel needed for effective decentralization.
- Issues regarding coordination with the European Union.
- Areas in which competencies should be centralized and areas in which competencies should be decentralized.

The full set of questions asked in the wrapup session and a summary of the discussions may be found in Appendix D of the companion volume.

Although we never asked participants' opinions of regionalization or their opinions about the proposed referendum, these opinions were from time to time expressed. These and other voluntary contributions germane to the discussion were noted and incorporated in our interpretation of the results of the four game sessions.

---

[21] This method of transcription was chosen to free up the rapporteur to attend fully to the dynamics of the discussion. The rapporteurs did keep their own "process notes" during the team meetings to record minority opinions and other features of the discussion that might enlighten our

CHAPTER 3: RESULTS

In this chapter, we will describe and discuss the results of the four seminar gaming sessions. Before focusing on the results, it is worthwhile to make a general comment on the conduct of the four sessions. As we noted in the previous chapter, not one of the 83 people who agreed to participate failed to attend. Knowledgability and a commitment to discuss issues accompanied this evidence of interest. Because the participants came with different viewpoints, the debate in the teams was intense, sometimes so much so that all the topics in the team tasking protocol could not be covered. However, despite this intensity, the participants took care to maintain an objective tone to the deliberations; disagreements were handled with respect for each other's viewpoints. In general, the participants indicated at the end of each day that they enjoyed playing the game; they found the experience to be creative, stimulating, valuable and fun. Based on their comments after the sessions, the likelihood is high that the participants left the seminar game sessions more empowered and more disposed to contribute to the regionalization debate in their respective communities and regions.

From the team deliberations and wrapup sessions, we have identified nine themes that played major roles; these will form the structure of this chapter. Some of the themes represent issues that were brought out in most (if not all) team discussions; others differed in relevance or nature for different scenarios or in different game locales. For each theme, we will first provide a capsule summary of the main point of the theme, followed by a description of the deliberations and a brief discussion of the meaning we take from those deliberations. Our interpretation is derived not only from game materials, but also from the interviews, the literature review, and the background knowledge possessed by the control team. These nine themes are:

A: Effect of the external scenarios;
B: Acceptance of the decentralization scenarios;
C: The importance of decentralization;
D: The best way to decentralize;
E: Distribution and coordination of responsibilities;
F: National government as the center of gravity in collection and distribution of financial resources;
G: The appropriate way to distribute financial resources over different layers of government;
H: Distribution of human resources over different layers of government;
I: National solidarity.

---

understanding of the deliberations. We view these process notes as confidential and therefore have not included them as part of the seminar game record provided in the companion volume.

A. EFFECT OF THE EXTERNAL SCENARIOS

The main point regarding the external scenarios was that they did not have a large effect. Mostly, when there were economic resources available, there was a tendency to try to solve problems by spending money. Scarcity of resources thus made the problems harder to solve.

Description

The external scenarios were presented to the players as plausible pictures of Portugal in 2010; any claim that they were predictions was explicitly disavowed. Following the presentation of the external scenario, participants were invited to react to it. Aside from some minor comments, there was remarkably little challenging of the scenario; players found it sufficiently plausible to accept it as the basis for further deliberations. Some comments indicated that players found the rainy scenario a bit more plausible than the sunny scenario; the large rate of annual growth was judged to be possible, but very optimistic.

This general assent by silence was modified somewhat by the behavior of the players in the team rooms. Teams confronted with the rainy scenario had a slightly more strained atmosphere during their deliberations; financial resources were not readily available to resolve problems or find compromises among different participant positions. Players searched the rainy scenario for positive aspects that could be used for developing policies. These were found, relieving any potential to be too pessimistic about this particular future. Teams confronted with the sunny scenario, on the other hand, were more relaxed and showed less concern about policy issues. Indeed, they appeared to pay less attention to the external scenario than their rainy scenario counterparts.

Discussion

In these seminar games, a favorable economic climate appeared to result in less concern about the way government was organized. In all of the decentralization scenarios, potential problems tended to be met by solutions based upon spending. Thus, the specific way that decentralization is accomplished may be more critical in difficult economic times than in prosperous ones, because it becomes more important to deal efficiently with available resources.

B. ACCEPTANCE OF THE DECENTRALIZATION SCENARIOS

The main point regarding this theme was that there was occasionally (not in all sessions) a small amount of difficulty accepting decentralization scenarios B and C. Each scenario met with its own objections. However, these difficulties were always overcome, and the decentralization scenarios were effectively employed in the participants' deliberations.

Description

In contrast to the external scenarios, there was more difficulty in accepting the decentralization scenarios. Generally, people were willing to accept Scenario A, probably because it was based upon well-publicized propositions put forth by the current government for creating administrative regions. Although the general concept of Scenario B was acceptable, and participants readily adopted the notion of decentralization, there was sometimes difficulty accepting competencies devolving to municipalities. In Lisboa, for example, one of the participants in Team B strongly objected to the possibility that municipalities would be able to accept and successfully manage the competencies posed in Scenario B. The rapporteur and other participants persevered in their discussion and this participant eventually accepted the scenario; we noted no residual disaffection in this person's further contributions. Although there was some fear on the part of the game designers that participants would have difficulty accepting a cancellation of the referendum in Scenario C, this problem did not arise. However, the participants did have problems with the unclear division of competencies in Scenario C.

In the wrapup session, there did not emerge any consensus as to whether Scenario A (a "yes" vote) or Scenario B (a "no" vote) was the better choice. Scenario C did not fare as well as the other two in this regard. Participants expressed difficulty understanding just what the structure in Scenario C would entail, and were therefore more reluctant to find benefits in it. This could be due to the inherent ambiguity in that scenario or to the greater familiarity of the participants with the first two scenarios.

Discussion

We attribute some of the resistance encountered with Scenario B to our deliberate efforts to not place all participants in decentralization scenarios they were known to favor. Thus, some members of the various Scenario B teams in the four cities were known to be in favor of regionalization and some were known to be opposed. The minor resistance we encountered is overshadowed by the general finding that all of the decentralization scenarios were accepted after discussion. Although specific elements of each scenario might encounter significant discussion, these elements varied from game session to game session; no point was subject to repeated heavy criticism.

C. THE IMPORTANCE OF DECENTRALIZATION

The main point regarding this theme was—as we have noted before—that there is a strong consensus among the participants in all four sessions for a decentralization of the Portuguese government. This does not mean that decentralization is viewed as a cure for all the ills of the country or as a benefit without drawbacks; however, the benefits—if decentralization is carefully implemented—are viewed as greatly outweighing the costs.

Description

Participants were explicit and virtually unanimous in their declaration that some decentralization of competencies is very important and necessary. The present Portuguese government was viewed as too centralist and no longer (if it ever was) the appropriate way to deal with problems in society. These emerged in all four game sessions and in all decentralization scenarios. In expressing this belief, several arguments were repeatedly heard.

- Most participants believed that decentralization will lead to a <u>more responsive</u> government because the government will be closer to the people. The current trend in society is that citizens get more demanding and want more accessibility to government.[22] Therefore the participants believe that an increasing part of the government activities needs to be carried out at a lower than national level.

- Most participants, especially those facing decentralization scenarios A and B, believed that decentralization would generally lead to a <u>more efficient</u> government because government would be more responsive to the demands of the people. In addition to decentralization, there are other factors—such as increased competition, privatization and development of information technology—that could contribute to a more efficient government.

---

[22] We view this as not only a general trend in Western Europe, but especially true in Portugal in the continuing aftermath of the 1974 overthrow of the dictatorship.

- Most participants, especially those facing decentralization scenarios B and C, believed that decentralization would lead to a <u>less bureaucratic</u> government. However, in scenario A there was no consensus on the effect of decentralization on bureaucracy.

- Most participants, especially those facing scenarios A and B, believed that decentralization would lead to <u>more quality</u> in government policymaking. Generally, the participants expected better management in specific policy areas. However, as we elaborate below, it is not exactly clear which policy areas would be managed better and which would be managed worse; different opinions were expressed both within and among teams.

The participants also pointed out that decentralization might have negative side effects. Decentralization might make it more difficult to accomplish structural changes and to formulate national policies. The participants believed that where competencies have national implications (e.g., water management, air quality, encouraging foreign tourism), conflicts of interest within Portugal might result in decentralized decision making being less effective. In these situations, policies might be based on considerations of a lowest common denominator rather than on overall benefit. This expression of concern was stronger in Scenarios A and C, where there was an explicit introduction of a new layer of government, with possibly little experience in policymaking. Another disadvantage to decentralization was its potential to magnify differences among different parts of the country, and hamper efforts to increase inter-regional equity (see below).

Relationships between Portugal and the EU were also believed to affect decentralization. It was strongly believed that Portugal needs to speak with one voice in Brussels, and decentralization (but especially regionalization) might make it more difficult to achieve that objective. The increased harmonization of policies through the European Union (emphasized in the sunny scenario but also present in the rainy scenario) was believed to reduce the options available to either a national or decentralized Portuguese policymaking body and could therefore make any structural change less important. For example, some participants viewed environmental policy as being taken over by the European Union and therefore not a major issue for subnational governmental units. Additionally, some participants expressed uncertainty regarding how decentralization would affect the relationships between neighboring Portuguese and Spanish municipalities. In Lisboa, for example, it was mentioned that some of the poorer parts of Portugal might prefer to link up with geographically adjacent Spanish regions instead of Portuguese ones.[23]

Although decentralization was generally judged positively, the participants agreed in the abstract that some competencies could be better dealt with at a national level and some at a lower level. Unfortunately, there was no agreement on the question which specific policy areas would benefit from decentralization and which would not. Generally, it seems that education (especially in Scenario A), spatial planning (especially in Scenario A), culture (especially in Scenario B) and sport (especially in Scenario B) would benefit from decentralization. Health care, however, was expected to worsen because of decentralization (especially in Scenario B and C). However, there was no agreement on this. According to the participants, the most important reason to deal with certain competencies at a national level is to preserve national cohesion (see Theme I).

Discussion

An assumption we made in designing the seminar game was that a "status quo" scenario with a highly centralized government would be roundly criticized and largely dismissed by the participants as ineffective. The results of the gaming sessions make clear that there is strong agreement on the fact that a more decentralized structure of government has many advantages over the current, overly centralized, government. This underscores our assumption; more benefit was obtained by employing the variety of reactions to three decentralization decisions than would have been obtained contrasting centralization to decentralization.

The deliberations brought out several aspects of the decentralization issue. Although it was believed that decentralization would lead to a more responsive, more efficient, less bureaucratic and high quality government, this was largely a matter of faith. As evidenced by the diversity of ways in which the participants believed these benefits would be realized, there is no certainty that decentralization will prove beneficial. Much depends on the implementation of any decentralization restructuring. That is, there are many possible ways to decentralize and there is no agreement on the best way to do it; it is possible that the specific form of decentralization is less important than the way in which that form is implemented.

---

[23] Probably because of the inherently internal nature of the regionalization issue, the participants did not spend much time discussing Portugal's relationships with other countries.

D. THE BEST WAY TO DECENTRALIZE

The main point regarding the best way to decentralize is that no clear direction emerged from the seminar games. Instead, any of the options presented by the decentralization scenarios could be successful, if it were effectively implemented. Thus, the choice among decentralization alternatives should be based more upon the quality and explicitness of their implementation plans than on predictions of their results.

Description

Although there was clear agreement on the question whether decentralization should take place, there was no agreement among the participants on what the best form of decentralization might be. Rather than ask participants which form they would prefer, we instead placed them in different decentralization scenarios, and asked them to provide a "best case" description of Portugal within their scenarios. In our presentation of each decentralization scenario, we deliberately attempted to induce a spirit of cooperation, so that even if individual participants were predisposed to believe that their particular decentralization method was not the best option, they would attempt to make the best of the situation. In this spirit, even people who expressed a firm prior belief that regionalization was not a good option could work with Scenario A and see benefits.

Regionalization, in the forms of Scenarios A and C, was viewed as enabling the different regions in Portugal to better take advantage of their specific characteristics. For example, participants in the Évora session stated that only regionalization will allow the Alentejo to become a producing region (the province cannot just be the country's nature reserve). More generally, according to some of the participants, regionalization will lead to a more balanced growth.

Regionalization might also have drawbacks, in addition to the ones mentioned for decentralization in Theme C. One of the most important possible drawbacks mentioned was that regionalization will create a new political middle class and will thus create a potential for conflict between elected bodies on different levels. More than once, participants commented that ambitious local officials will see regionalization as a chance to upgrade their own political careers. Another possible drawback might be that some types of regionalization, such as the one described in Scenario C (i.e. vague distribution of responsibilities over national, regional and local government), will not lead to more efficiency.

The participants mentioned that some effects of regionalization are hard to foresee. For example, it is not clear what the establishment of administrative regions in the mainland will mean for the position of the autonomous regions of the Azores and Madeira.

Some participants believe that local government is the right level to do things because municipalities and parishes know better what the people want. In Porto, a clear majority of the participants appears to have a strong preference for the transfer of powers to the municipalities instead of regionalization. But even there, a possible drawback of transferring powers to the municipalities (it might encourage corruption) was also mentioned.

Discussion

While the participants believe there is a clear need for decentralization in Portugal, it appears that either regionalization or devolution to municipalities could work. The arguments presented for or against regionalization were not as important to the participants as the need for clarity in the way in which any particular form of decentralization would be implemented. This is not merely a choice among the lesser of evils; our participants were able to see positive sides to all three alternatives. To choose for regionalization or not, one must first assure that any particular plan is capable of being implemented, and then consider in more detail the goals of decentralization. To the extent that the goals of regionalization are ambiguous (such as vaguely stating a preference for governmental efficiency), it is hard to assess the comparative value of different structures. The deliberations regarding Scenario C emphasize this point, where our induction to "do the best with what you have" was least able to be achieved.

The central idea of this theme may be illustrated by considering the problem commonly expressed in Portugal that citizens often face a maze of bureaucracy which makes it difficult for them to find out which office they need to go for specific information or with specific problems; in the countryside, this can mean travelling from town to town to deal with different governmental departments. Advocates of regionalization argue that administrative regions will solve this problem by providing a more coherent governmental structure. This was viewed as an outcome in the deliberations within Scenario A. However, such coherence also emerged in the self-organizing coalitions of municipalities in Scenario B and the regional decision centers of Scenario C. Regionalization might be a way to ease the burden on bureaucracy, but it is not the only way.

E. DISTRIBUTION AND COORDINATION OF RESPONSIBILITIES

The main point of this theme is that as competencies are moved from a central government to local or even private authorities, coordination becomes a critical need. Although most of the public discussion has been about <u>vertical</u> coordination (central government to regions or municipalities), <u>horizontal</u> coordination (among regions or municipalities) is of at least equal importance. The debate focuses too much on government, and thereby misses the potential role of the private sector as an element of decentralization.

Description

Team deliberations, especially in Question Set 2, concentrated on the need for coordination of government policies. All discussions concluded that a clear definition of responsibilities is an important condition for efficient and effective coordination. In Scenarios A and C, all 13 competencies that were proposed for regionalization require shared responsibilities; they touch on regional and local government, but need involvement of the central government. Sometimes, this was viewed to be over-governance, as specific tasks might be better dealt with autonomously (by a region or municipality).

Although most of the discussion on governmental coordination with respect to decentralization concentrated on vertical coordination (from central to local, possibly with regions), the teams also brought out the need for horizontal coordination—among regions or among municipalities. In Scenario B, the absence of administrative regions meant that municipalities had to manage their own horizontal coordination; this led to participants discussing a need for the central government to offer assistance and to serve as arbitrator if horizontal coordination failed. In Scenarios A and C, the administrative regions themselves were viewed as needing horizontal coordination; again, the central government had a role. The regional administrations, however, took over the central governmental role of arbitrating the horizontal coordination among municipalities.

Vertical vs. horizontal coordination was not viewed as a uniform matter. A criterion for the need for vertical coordination is shared responsibilities. When responsibility can be pushed downwards (spatial planning was mentioned as an example), then horizontal coordination is more important.

For some competencies, vertical coordination is important. Even if the competency has devolved to the lower level of government, the higher level must be active in setting guidelines and monitoring compliance with these guidelines. Frequently mentioned examples of competencies requiring vertical coordination were health care, education and employment.

For other competencies, there is a predominant need for horizontal coordination, and the higher levels of government need not be involved except in the arbitration role mentioned above. Examples of competencies that, according to the participants, require horizontal coordination, are spatial planning and water supply.

In keeping with the belief in the need for decentralization, participants generally favored vertical subsidiarity. Sometimes even in Scenarios A and C, the participants would want to move competencies from regional administration to municipalities or even (less frequently) parishes.

Participants also introduced a different form of horizontal subsidiarity—i.e., the transfer of responsibilities to organizations outside the government. In most of the teams, privatization was heavily discussed. The participants believed that the central government could gain in efficiency, effectiveness and quality if various services would be privatized (regardless of regionalization). Although most participants favored privatization, only few examples of competencies eligible for privatization were given. In Évora in Scenario B, it was mentioned that improvements in the areas of culture, environment and infrastructure are expected because of the introduction of private initiatives in the Alentejo.

It is important to determine which government tasks could be (better) done by organizations outside the government, and to examine each instance in detail. Thus, privatization was viewed as an attractive option on the surface, but needed to be carefully examined before it was undertaken.

Discussion

In a situation in which governmental responsibilities are moved around, the examination of new mechanisms for vertical and horizontal coordination is important in order to develop balanced and consistent policies. The definition and development of explicit mechanisms for both need to be part of a decentralization plan. This emerged from all three decentralization scenarios and in all four game sessions. The issue is most critical when one considers the transfer of responsibilities as a decentralization plan is implemented.

F. NATIONAL GOVERNMENT AS THE CENTER OF GRAVITY IN COLLECTION AND DISTRIBUTION OF FINANCIAL RESOURCES

The main point of this theme is that the participants do not see any change in the predominant role of the central government as the collector and distributor of financial resources. Although the local governments will have more authority and responsibility for the <u>spending</u> of money, equity and efficiency demand that the <u>collecting</u> should remain a central responsibility.

Description

An obvious but important conclusion is that the offices that are responsible for the decentralized activities should have sufficient money to perform the tasks appointed to them. This could be arranged in two different ways. Firstly, more money could be transferred from the national to sub-national levels of government. Secondly, the sub-national levels of government could be offered the possibility to collect money. All of the seminar game sessions made clear that most participants have a strong preference for the first option. That is, the national government should be the principal party for the distribution of money over different layers of government. A logical consequence is that the national government should remain responsible for the collection of financial resources.

The participants agreed that a substantial increase in the amount of money transferred to local or regional levels of government is needed. Currently, local governments receive approximately eight percent of revenues, one of the lowest percentages in Europe. There appeared to be a consensus that the distribution of money should be dictated by a national formula, in order to keep the financial and fiscal structure of government transparent.[24] If the regions or municipalities would be able to create different taxes with different rates, the system would become too confusing. Although the participants agreed that the distribution of money should be dictated by a national formula, they did not suggest a concrete formula. Numbers mentioned as appropriate percentages of total revenues for local use ranged from 10 to 40, and there was no convergence to any central figure.

Nobody believed that the way government is financed needed to change greatly. "Big" taxes (VAT, income tax, property tax, etc.) should continue to be collected at a national level. In addition, local governments should have some freedom in raising revenues through small items such as service fees. There appeared to be agreement

---

[24] The present Portuguese government does use formulas for distribution of resources, but these were never mentioned in any of the sessions.

on the fact that regions (if they would be established) and municipalities should have little or no possibilities to collect money by means of new taxes.

Discussion

The participants agreed that a precondition for effective decentralization is a substantial shift in public monies to local levels of government (meaning regions if they exist, municipalities, and parishes) is needed. There is a consensus over all three scenarios that there needs to be a formula determined at the national level to determine how much money each local unit will receive. That having been said, the local unit would have more autonomy in deciding how to spend the money it received.

When decentralization takes place, money will have to be transferred from the national to local levels of government. Part of this money should come from cutbacks in the expenditures of the central government.[25] It will, however, not be easy to reduce central government spending on all matters that are transferred to the regions, because many of these involve shared responsibilities—i.e., the tasks are of a consultative nature or involve cooperation with the central government.

Thus far, it is not yet clear what the financial consequences of decentralization (much less regionalization) will be. This topic is more or less absent from the debate on regionalization.

G. WHAT IS THE APPROPRIATE WAY TO DISTRIBUTE FINANCIAL RESOURCES OVER DIFFERENT LAYERS OF GOVERNMENT?

The main point of this theme is that every level of government is entitled to a budget adequate to the responsibilities it carries. If local governments must bargain amongst themselves or with higher authorities for funding, then they have neither competency nor dignity.

Description

In the previous theme, we noted that it was stressed in all sessions that a single national formula is desirable to determine exactly what amount of money goes to the different decentralized governing units. Here, we explore this major issue in more detail.

---

[25] In addition, economic growth will make more money available to the government which can be transferred to lower levels of government.

The participants stressed that it is important that each layer of government is assured of a certain amount of money. Even at the level of the parish, there is a need to know what amount of money they will obtain. There should be a transparent system for the distribution of financial resources over all of the different layers of government, so that decentralized governance can function autonomously and does not have to ask for money from a higher level. Furthermore, it was agreed that the national formula itself should contain some kind of mechanism to correct for regional imbalances. The majority of the participants indicated that some flexibility should remain in addition to this single national formula. There was, however, no agreement on the question how exactly this flexibility should be crystallized. Several possibilities were suggested.

A first suggestion was that each local level of government (e.g., regions or municipalities) should have some freedom to transfer part of their resources to the next lower level of government (e.g., municipalities or parishes, respectively) by means of agreements (hierarchically). However, not everybody agreed, because this would make the system less transparent and political discrimination might occur.

A second suggestion was to create funds within the national government which local governments access when they need money for special projects. This suggestion required a mechanism to decide which local units would have access under what circumstances. Fault was found with this suggestion because it could create too much competitiveness among units and hamper horizontal coordination.

Most participants indicated that the local government, once it has the money, needs autonomy (within guidelines, perhaps) in how to spend it.

Discussion

Whether a particular form of decentralization is good or not depends to a substantial extent on the way the local government will be financed. This means that a regionalization proposal offered to the country needs to contain some idea about how the national formula is determined, and what the guidelines for autonomy might be. In Scenario B, participants assumed that the manner of transferring funds from the central government to municipalities would generally continue, even as the amounts themselves increased. However, in Scenario A (which followed the referendum) and Scenario C, there was no information on the composition of the national formula (because it has not been clear in the public debate on regionalization). Hence, the participants were not able to judge what the likely effects on the functioning of government would be. This would also likely hold for voters when the referendum is put before them.

H. DISTRIBUTION OF HUMAN RESOURCES OVER DIFFERENT LAYERS OF GOVERNMENT

The main point of this theme is that decentralization of competencies must be accompanied by qualified people to administer at the local levels. For some localities and some competencies, there should be shortages in qualified personnel.

Description

The participants were not specifically asked to indicate what decentralization in general or regionalization specifically would mean for the distribution of human resources. Nevertheless, some important remarks in this respect were made.

Strategic resources do not only include the institutions, but also the actors. An important point of discussion was whether there are sufficient skilled workers to fill newly created jobs at a regional or local level. It was mentioned that it is implausible that the number of civil servants will not increase when decentralization will take place.

Discussion

The quality of the government policy mainly depends on the quality of the people. One could expect the quality of people to increase because of improvements in the level of education. On the other hand, the need for highly educated people increases when the number of decision-making levels increases. And, in addition, people cannot be forced to go work for regional or local government offices when they are working for the national government.

When thinking about decentralization, it is very important to consider what kind of personnel is needed on all levels of government and whether this personnel is available. Thus far, it seems that this topic has not yet received much attention in the debate on regionalization.

I. NATIONAL SOLIDARITY

The main point of this theme is that the participants expressed the strong opinion that decentralization should not diminish the national solidarity of the Portuguese people. Decentralization and national solidarity are not necessarily mutually exclusive, but care must be taken that devolution does not result in divisiveness.

Description

The participants agreed that regionalization should not lead to increasing differences among or within regions. They expressed some fear that differences among regions might increase in some areas such as socio-economic status and access to health care. Therefore, mechanisms should be put in place to ensure national solidarity and cohesion.

This fear was more strongly expressed in the rainy scenario than in the sunny one. When money is available, transfers from rich areas to poor areas are not much of a problem. But when money is tight, such transfers may be problematic.

A further fear regarding solidarity was expressed in Scenario C, where the metropolitan areas of Lisboa and Porto had explicit standing as centers for decision making. Participants in the Évora and Viseu sessions expressed fear that in such circumstances, equitable sharing of money would be harder.

Apart from the differences among regions themselves, regionalization might have different effects on different groups in Portuguese society. Some comments in this regard arose spontaneously, and some when the participants were asked in Question Set 4 to indicate how decentralization would effect small and medium enterprises (SMEs), large industrial firms, unskilled and semi-skilled laborers, retirees and people desiring to preserve Portuguese cultural and natural heritage.[26] According to the participants, SMEs will probably be better off because they will receive help from specific support bodies within each region. The participants think SMEs will probably have better prospects thanks to easier contacts and thus an easier start-up process. New products, which will be the banner for each region, will create opportunities. However, the regions will have less power than central government to really do things. Large industrial firms will not be greatly effected by regionalization. Because they have to deal with new governmental entities, they will have to change their operating philosophy, but they will be able to do so. The beliefs regarding SMEs were related to assumptions about which competencies decentralized government could handle easily. The better the capability of decentralized government to manage economic growth, the better off were SMEs, as the local authorities could tailor conditions to specific needs. On the other hand, if local governments were not capable of such management, SMEs could suffer compared to their fate in the current centralized regime.

---

[26] Recall that some teams in some game sessions did not have time to answer these questions. Therefore, this description is based on only some of the teams.

There was no consensus on the impact of regionalization on unskilled and semi-skilled laborers. Some participants believed that they might be slightly better off, while others expressed the opinion that they might be slightly worse off. Neither side believed that there would be major changes in the position of these groups. The participants believed that retirees will probably be slightly better off, because of improved social support for retirees.

The national cultural and natural heritages were seen as benefiting from regionalization according to the participants in Scenario A. The main mechanism mentioned was that people care more for assets close to home. A counterargument mentioned by some was that attention to culture and natural heritages may suffer in the competition for further economic development.

A topic that was addressed regularly in the discussions within the teams, especially in Scenario B, was the possibility of increasing tensions within the Portuguese society. According to the participants, tensions might arise between immigrants and natives, employed and unemployed (classes), old and young (competition for resources; rise of a new youth culture) and people living in urban and rural areas. The participants indicated that there is a danger that social and cultural ghettos will emerge and that violence and isolation will increase, especially in larger cities. Although this is more an effect of "natural evolution" than of regionalization, regionalization might affect how such potential conflicts are addressed.

Discussion

Central government has an important role in monitoring the effect of regionalization on the differences between regions and has to undertake action to mitigate any such differences. Without special attention to this potential problem, there is a large danger that regionalization (if it came to exist) would lead to larger differences among regions because of different resources available to the regions. It was mentioned, for example, that compensation mechanisms are needed to guarantee proper education in the whole country. A counterargument to this belief (expressed by a few participants) was that regionalization might lead to more responsiveness in the form of a better approach to handling conflicts. The resulting lessening of tensions would serve to strengthen national solidarity. But whatever the viewpoint regarding the direction of regionalization, all participants were united on the importance of maintaining solidarity.

CHAPTER 4: IMPLICATIONS FOR THE REGIONALIZATION DEBATE

The major objective of the seminar gaming exercise reported here is to inform the debate surrounding the forthcoming referendum on regionalization. Perhaps the most important finding in this regard is the often-stated remark by participants that improvements in the information supply with respect to the referendum are necessary. A number of participants criticized the government and the largest opposition party alike for poorly managing the referendum process. These critics stated that there has not yet been a serious debate on regionalization in Portugal, and the public has not yet been given sufficient information to make an informed choice. These and other participants indicated that—in spite of the wording of the referendum and the interpretation of that wording stated by the Constitutional Court of Portugal—it is not clear to them what the actual proposal is. If these motivated and informed citizens hold such a belief, then the average voter, even trying to be informed, is not likely to know what he or she is voting for. A possible consequence is a high abstention rate, making the results of the referendum inconclusive and further clouding the national debate.

REGIONALIZATION—YES OR NO?

A major finding of our study is that everybody seems to be in favor of decentralization. However, there is no consensus about whether decentralization should be accomplished by the implementation of the referendum proposal (Scenario A), direct devolution to municipalities (Scenario B) or horizontally coordinated regional decision centers (Scenario C). Before taking decisions on the best way to decentralize, it has to be clear which objectives are to be reached by the decentralization process. Subsequently, the type of decentralization that will most likely contribute to reaching those objectives may be chosen.

One issue to consider in this regard is the level of decentralization. Most governments have different organizational layers to which responsibilities can be transferred, meaning that government responsibilities can be decentralized in a variety of ways. In Portugal, a first option is to transfer powers from a national to a currently-existing local level (as in Scenario B). A second option is to transfer powers from the national government to one of the existing intermediate levels of government, i.e. to strengthen a currently-existing governmental entity between the national and current local levels. These could be an empowerment of the present 18 administrative districts or the present five CCRs (or their modification as in Scenario C). A third option is to establish a new layer of government to which responsibilities can be transferred (as in Scenario A). This question has been the central one in the regionalization debate in Portugal to date.

The seminar games indicated that the question may not be as critical as some people believe, in the sense that feasible ways to implement many different forms of decentralization are possible. The referendum is focused on only one particular form of decentralization—as embodied in Laws 56/91 and 19/98—and this is perhaps unfortunate. The details of that particular form, which include the number and location of the regions and the establishment of the directly elected regional assembly, mask the essential question of the functioning of any regional administrative body and how such a body would exercise its competencies and interact with both the central government and its constituent municipalities.

KNOWLEDGE TO INFORM AN ELECTORATE

Our answer to the question about regionalization in the subsection above is "it depends." Here, we indicate what it depends upon.

The devil is in the details.

The seminar game made clear that the <u>implementation</u> of any decentralization scheme is at least as important as the actual characteristics of the scheme itself. Regionalization as a plan will succeed or fail depending on how it is implemented. This information—possibly premature—is certainly absent. Because the public is to be asked to give its opinion on the specific scheme of Laws 56/91 and 19/98 rather than on the abstract question of some form of regional administration, the implementation details must be provided to inform that vote. Proponents of the referendum should make clear which steps are to be taken and in what time frame. The schedule for devolving competencies and the horizontal and vertical coordination plans must be made explicit. And the financial structure to support all of this must be presented in detail.

Money does matter.

One of the details not discussed in the present regionalization debate is how the new form of government will be financed. Our participants agreed that the financial structure of Portuguese taxation should not change, and that there should be a national formula to determine the share of each identified local unit. Moreover, they

agreed that more money must be made available to local government to spend.
While the details of the national formula (distribution plan) need not be part of the
referendum debate, attention should be paid to the amount of money to be available
to regional administration (and in turn to municipalities and parishes) and the
autonomy in spending that money that the regional administrations would have. We
also believe that the debate would benefit by the provision of a general philosophy to
be used in drawing up the national formula for distribution. This philosophy should
be explicit about the meaning of equity, the expectations placed upon richer and
poorer regions, how special needs would be considered, and how adjustments might
be made for economically good or bad times.

Competencies do matter.

Ambiguities exist in the regionalization plan proposed in the referendum not only
with respect to the allocation of financial resources, but also regarding the how
competencies would devolve. An important consideration here is the form of
devolution. Decentralization of a specific responsibility to a specific layer of
government can take different forms. The most important distinction is whether
responsibilities are fully decentralized (autonomy) or are shared between different
levels of government (shared responsibilities). This distinction needs to be explicit
in the consideration of the role of a regional administration. The electorate would be
well-served by more information regarding how competencies would be transferred
to regions, including an overview of the coordination mechanisms for the different
competencies, a plan for the distribution of financial and human resources and a
consideration of mechanisms to fight the asymmetries that might result from
regionalization.

BEYOND THE REFERENDUM

The different types of decentralization have different effects on the functioning of the
government. While there is not one "best" type, some options will work better than
others, depending on the objectives the government wants to reach with
decentralization and on the mechanisms put in place to avoid or correct possible
negative side-effects of decentralization. Even though there is a strong consensus for
decentralization, we must caution that decentralization—via regionalization or other
means—will not automatically have positive effects. Certain conditions need to be
met to make decentralization succeed. These conditions (such as a clear division of

responsibilities, a clear distribution of financial and human resources and national cohesion) were discussed above.

Whatever the outcome of the referendum, and whatever decentralization scheme is adopted by Portugal, a system needs to be put in place to evaluate the effects of decentralization. It is virtually certain that implementation will not be perfect—that some things will work well and others not so well. It could happen that decentralization has the desired consequences, but, in addition, has some foreseen or unforeseen negative side-effects. Mechanisms should be put in place to avoid or mitigate any negative direct effects or side-effects. An evaluation system, keyed to explicit objectives, will permit the monitoring of changes, and will permit Portugal to adaptively adjust its plan. If it turns out that regionalization indeed results in reaching the defined objectives, further steps to regionalize will be taken. If some (or all) objectives are not reached, perhaps alternative forms of decentralization for some competencies may need to be considered. By taking such an attentive, adaptive approach, Portugal can best ensure that decentralization is accomplished in an efficient, orderly manner.

BIBLIOGRAPHY

BOOKS AND REPORTS

Comissão de Coordenação da Região do Norte, *Contributos para o Debate Sobre Regionalização/Descentralização Administrativa,* Porto, Janeiro de 1997.

Departamento de Prospectiva e Planeamento, *Cenário da Evolução Estrutural da Economia Portuguesa 1995 -2015,* Lisboa, Maio de 1995.

Departamento de Prospectiva e Planeamento, *Três cenários para a Economia Portuguesa no Horizonte 2010/2015*, Lisboa, Versão de Janeiro de 1998.

Direcção Geral do Ordenamento do Território e Desenvolvimento Urbano, *Georeferenciação de Áreas Urbanas, Turísticas e Industriais,* Lisboa, Maio de 1998.

Economist, *Pocket Europe in Figures,* London, 1997.

Gaspar, J., *The Regions of Portugal,* Ministry of Planning and Administration of the Territory, Lisbon, 1993.

Ministério da Educação, Gabinete de Estudos e Planeamento, *Critérios de Planeamento da Rede Escolar,* Lisboa, 1990.

Ministério da Educação, Departamento de Programação e Gestão Financeira, *Portuguese Education System: Situation and Trends 1992,* Lisboa, 1995.

Ministério da Educação, Departamento de Avaliação, Prospectiva e Planeamento, *Ano Escolar 1997/98: Estatísticas Preliminares,* Lisboa, 1997.

Ministério do Equipamento, Planeamento e da Administração do Território, Direcção-Geral da Administração Autárquica, *Serviços Desconcentrados de Âmbito Regional,* Lisboa, Janeiro de 1998.

Ministério do Planeamento e da Administração do Território, Direcção-Geral do Desenvolvimento Regional, *Fundos Estruturais 10 Anos,* Lisboa, Setembro de 1995.

Opello, W.C., Jr., *Portugal's Political Development: A Comparative Approach,* Westview Press/Boulder and London, 1985.

Pinto, A.C., *Modern Portugal,* The Society for the Promotion of Science and Scholarship, Palo Alto, California, 1998.

NEWSPAPER ARTICLES

Espada, J.C., "Regionalização e Estado-nação", *O Público,* 2 Dezembro de 1996.

Ferreira, L., "Regionalização Afecta Próximo QCA", *Público Economia,* 16 Dezembro de 1997.

Moreira, V., "Centralismo Primário", *Espaço Público,* 13 Janeiro de 1998.

Moreira, V., "Lições do Primeiro Referendo", *Espaço Público,* 30 Junho de 1998.

Oliveira, I., "Regionalização em Curso", *O Independente,* 9 Abril de 1998.

Pereira, R.N., "A Grande Oportunidade do Porto", *Diário Económico,* 13 Outubro de 1997.

Pereira, R.N., "Transferências Regionais Beneficiam Algarve", *Diário Económico*, 27 Outubro de 1997.

Xavier, A.L., "Autonomia Regional e Regionalização", *Espaço Público*, 8 Janeiro de 1997.

Xavier, A.L., "Variações Sobre a Regionalização", *Espaço Público*, 21 Maio de 1997.

White, D., and P. Wise, "Portuguese Banking and Finance: Confident of a Strong Start in EMU", *Financial Times*, 8 April 1998.

INTERNET PAGES

American Embassy in Portugal, *Investment Climate Statement*, http://www.american-embassy.pt/wwwhecon.html

Eduvinet, *Transformation of Society in Portugal and Integration into the EEC*, http://www.merian.fr.bw.schule.de/eduvinet/port001.htm

Interview with Jorge Sampaio, Portuguese President and Former COR Member, http://europa.eu.int/comreg/pr/jorgesen.html

National Association of Portuguese Municipalities, *The Structure of Local Authorities in Portugal*, http://www.anmp.pt/en/index1.html

OECD, *Issues and Developments in Public Management: Survey 1996-1997 on Portugal*, http://www.oecd.org/puma/gvrnance/surveys/pubs/report97/surveypt.htm

OECD, *Economic Survey of Portugal February 1998*, http://www.oecd.org/eco/surv/ esu-por.htm

OECD, *OECD in Figures - Education*, http://www.oecd.org/publications/figures/educ.html

PortugalNet, *The Portuguese Economy*, http://www.portugalnet.pt/negocio/buying/ 021tpe.html

Stranmill College Belfast, *Education Structure - Portugal*, http://www.stran.ni.ac.uk/ pages/ed-structs/port-struct.html

Tradecompass, *Portugal: Economic Trends and Outlook*, http://www.tradecompass.com/ library/books/com_guide/portugal02.html